Delia's Kitchen Garden

A BEGINNERS' GUIDE TO GROWING AND COOKING FRUIT AND VEGETABLES

BBC BOOKS

Delia's
Kitchen Garden

9 8 7 6 5 4 3 2

Published in 2007 by BBC Books, an imprint of Ebury Publishing.
First published in Great Britain by BBC Books in 2004.

Ebury Publishing is a division of the Random House Group.

A proportion of the recipes in this book has been previously published in *Delia
Smith's Complete Illustrated Cookery Course*, *Delia Smith's Complete Cookery Course*,
Delia Smith's Christmas, *Delia Smith's Winter Collection*, *Delia Smith's Summer
Collection*, *Delia's How To Cook Books One* and *Two*, *Delia's Vegetarian Collection*, *The
Delia Collection: Italian* and *Soup*, *Delia's Christmas Easy 2003*, Delia's website
www.deliaonline.com, and *Sainsbury's Magazine*

Edited for BBC Books by New Crane Publishing Ltd
Photographs Debbie Patterson
Photograph (page 68) © Debbie Patterson/Homes and Gardens/IPC Syndication
Extra photographs (Patio Garden and Square Foot Garden)/Tony Laryea

Design © New Crane Publishing Ltd 2004

The Random House Group Limited Reg. No. 954009
Addresses for companies within the Random House Group can be found at
www.randomhouse.co.uk

A CIP catalogue record for this book is available from the British Library.

Printed and bound in Great Britain by Butler & Tanner Ltd, Frome, Somerset
Colour separation by Butler & Tanner Ltd

ISBN 978 0 563 49373 0

Introduction

A few years ago, I was given the most inspired birthday present. 'Close your eyes tight,' said my husband, Michael, after he had walked me down to the end of our cottage garden. 'Turn around three times. One, two, three, open! That's it! That's your present!' But what? Where? All I could see was a field of corn in front of me.

And that was precisely it, stretching out in front of me, to left and right: a 6½-acre field. As birthday presents go, what a cracker. You see, since we had first moved to Suffolk, I had had a dream that if ever we owned the field, we could return it to the wild. Luckily, I have some friends, who are designers, who undertook the task: planting trees, recreating meadow land with wild flowers, and constructing a small lake. And – well, this is actually the point of all this – with their help, we realised another unfulfilled dream: a kitchen garden. Not just any kitchen garden, but an old-fashioned, walled kitchen garden.

Can you imagine anything more fitting for someone who cooks? Real vegetables, fruit and salads grown, not for commercial cropability, but for real flavour. I know what you're thinking: Delia? Gardening? Actually, no. I'm not a gardener but, Gay Search, who has been a close friend since my first date with Michael is. So, off we went, to rediscover the tradition of growing and cooking and enjoying good food. DELIA SMITH

There has never been a better time to grow your own fruit and vegetables. As we become more and more interested in what we eat, flavour becomes increasingly important and there is no doubt that freshly harvested, home-grown produce tastes so much better than anything you can buy in a shop. With government campaigns to persuade us, on health grounds, to eat five portions of fresh fruit and vegetables every day, it becomes a pleasure not a duty when you grow them yourself. If you have never grown anything before, I promise you, you will get such a buzz, not only from seeing the first seedlings appear, but from being able to harvest and enjoy the produce.

If you have read the recent revelations about the chemicals used in producing bags of prepared salad, you won't be surprised that we decided to grow our crops organically – feeding the soil with compost or manure and using no pesticides or other chemicals. Yes, you may get some holes in your cabbage leaves, but just cut out the damaged bits – it will taste just as good! Delia's kitchen garden was built with old brick paths around the beds, which are edged with wooden planks and, given how much space there is around it, we were also able to put up a fruit cage for soft fruit, and plant a small orchard with Delia's favourite Bramleys, pears and quinces.

But you don't have to have lots of space. You can grow crops anywhere – in a dedicated vegetable plot in the back garden or in among the ornamental plants in your borders. For those of you who have less space, there's our patio vegetable garden with everything growing in pots. And for those of you with tiny gardens – a Square Foot Garden – growing one crop per square foot of soil, where you can have as many or as a few as you can find room for.

We began our project in Delia's garden in the early spring because that's the time for getting a whole range of crops underway, but kitchen gardening is a 12-month cycle, so you can start at almost any time of the year sowing or planting – and even in the depths of winter you can always browse through a selection of seed catalogues and start ordering something.

Since Delia is away so much – something to do with some ball game, I believe – and I live in London, we relied heavily on Graham Baker, who lives near Delia, to keep the garden going day by day and to help out with the jobs where two pairs of hands are better than one. Without him, we would not have had the abundant harvest that we did.

I hope you'll be inspired by this book to have a go yourself. Even if you're just growing a few runner beans up a fence or some cut-and-come-again salads in a pot, you'll be delighted by how easy it is and how fabulous your crops taste. GAY SEARCH

Contents

Getting started

Equipment

There is a vast amount of gardening equipment available but, if you are just starting out, there are only a few essentials that you need. As with most things, you get what you pay for, so with tools that will last a lifetime go for the best you can afford. Stainless-steel tools, for instance, are a pleasure to dig with as the soil doesn't stick to them

Preparing the soil

Hoe *(opposite, from left)* Useful for weeding between rows of vegetables and marking out drills for sowing seeds, but not essential in a small plot.

Rake Use it for levelling the soil before sowing and for removing stones and other debris.

Spade and fork There are different sizes, with shafts of different lengths and handles of varying shapes. Go for one you feel comfortable with.

Trowel and hand fork A trowel is very useful for making holes when you are planting out seedlings. A hand fork is ideal for weeding.

Bucket *(second shelf)* A wheelbarrow substitute for the small plot. Use to carry compost, remove weeds and waste to the compost bin and when you harvest. If you have a large plot and room to store one, buy a wheelbarrow – as solidly built as you can afford.

Watering can *(top shelf)* Essential for watering drills before sowing, which you can't do with a hose. There are many different types in metal and plastic. My favourite is the NuCan (see page 165), which has a push button to open and close the spout, allowing you to water your plants and seedlings accurately.

Garden line *(top shelf, next to watering can)* Essential for getting your rows straight. Buy one or make one with two canes and twine.

Sowing seeds

Plastic seed trays and pots *(top shelf, centre)* For sowing seeds to be pricked out into individual pots later. Half trays are more useful than full trays for smaller quantities of plants, where space is limited.

Clear plastic propagator lids *(second shelf, next to bucket)* These speed up germination either in a greenhouse or on a windowsill.

Module trays *(third shelf, centre)* For individual seedlings or small clusters, which can be planted out later without disturbing the roots.

Biodegradable pots and Jiffy 7s *(fourth shelf, next to hand fork)* These are planted out into the soil with the seedling when it's large enough – this way, there is no disturbance at all to the root system.

Labels *(fourth shelf, in pot)* To mark what is where.

Dibber *(next to labels)* Made of wood or stainless steel, it's used to make small holes for young plants. Use a small one to prick out seedlings.

Protecting the crops

Cloches These can vary in shape from tent to bell or even tunnel and can be made of glass, plastic *(on ground, far right)* or polyurethane. Or, you can use a floating cloche – horticultural fleece *(in crate, on ground, centre)* laid over plants. The object is the same – to protect the plants from cold and bring forward or extend the cropping season.

Protective cages To protect crops against flying pests – butterflies, moths or birds. A framework can be made with ball joints *(in crate)* and dowelling or bamboo canes *(far right),* covered with enviromesh.

Training fruit

Galvanised wire and vine eyes *(third shelf)* Screw vine eyes into the mortar between bricks or into fence posts, then pull the wire tightly between them.

Bamboo canes Don't tie the branches of the fruit trees directly on to the wire. Attach them to canes, which are then tied on to the wires.

Secateurs *(top shelf)* Use to prune fruit trees. Go for the best and have them sharpened once a year.

Twine For tying branches and canes on to wires.

Groundwork

Before you start growing in earnest, there are a few basic jobs to be done, including getting the soil ready so your seedlings have the best chance of success, and building a compost bin

TASKS

Dig over the soil in the beds

Remove weeds, roots and large stones

Dig and prepare trenches

Build a compost bin

Layer the compost bin

Preparing the soil

The first job to do in the kitchen garden is to dig over the soil and remove all traces of weeds – not just the top growth but, more importantly, the roots. Most weeds can re-grow from just the smallest amount of root left in the soil and you do not want weeds competing with your crops for water, nutrients and even light. At the same time, remove any large stones from the soil. How you dig depends on what your soil is like.

If it's reasonably light and easy to work with, you need go down to only a spade's depth. Tackle the digging logically: start at one end of your chosen plot and dig a trench, piling the soil into a wheelbarrow or on to a ground sheet. Then spread some well-rotted manure or compost, which are rich in nutrients, along the bottom of the trench. Later on, you can use your own compost, but for now buy it from your local garden centre. Manure, too, can be bought from your local centre, or farms and riding stables are also good sources – some will even let you have it free if you cart it away yourself. Two spadefuls of compost, or one of manure, is enough for 1sq m (10.8sq ft) of soil. Don't be tempted to add an extra bit for good luck. If you make the soil too rich, your plants will produce growth that is very soft and sappy and it will act as a magnet for all the neighbourhood's pests.

When you have prepared the first trench, start digging a second one parallel to the first. Break up the soil as you pile it into the first trench, covering the compost. Carry on like this to the end of the plot, and then put the soil from the first trench into the last. If you have heavy clay soil, which sticks together like plasticine when wet and bakes as hard as concrete when dry, digging will be quite hard work and you will need to break up the soil in the bottom of the trenches with a fork to its full depth and mix in compost or manure, or even fine grit, to improve drainage. On really heavy clay, growing potatoes is an effective, no-work way to improve the soil structure because the roots and growing tubers will break it up for you. So concentrate on potatoes in the first year and in the second it will be easier to grow other crops. (If you're unsure whether your soil is clay, try moulding it into a ball – if you can, then you have clay soil.)

MAKING A COMPOST BIN

1 The bins for Delia's kitchen garden were made with 10cm (4in) square, pressure-treated timber posts at each corner, and 15cm (6in) planks.

2 We attached the planks to the post with stainless-steel screws, using a cordless drill.

3 The easiest way to fix the back planks to the posts at each end is with them lying flat on the ground. Ideally, make sure there's a tiny gap between the planks – no more than 5mm (¼in) – to allow air into the heap, but not enough to dry it out.

4 Raise the back section up, then screw one bottom side plank to the back post, and attach the other end to the front post.

5 With one right angle now made, the structure supports itself while you attach the other side planks. Do the other side in the same way.

6 Make sure the middle vertical post at the back is off-centre so that when the central planks dividing the bin into two are attached, they will be in the middle.

7 Two battens are attached to the insides of the front posts, creating a groove in which the individual front planks can slide up and down, making it very easy to get at the compost.

8 Stain the bins with a wood preservative – we opted for a mossy green colour.

LAYERING THE COMPOST BIN

The compost mix

1 To start off, you need a layer at the bottom that will allow air in – 15-20cm (6-8in) of woody, twiggy prunings will do the trick. They will eventually rot down, but not for a year or two. After the prunings, add the following layers:

2 'Browns' (these can sometimes be green!), which will also help to introduce air into the bottom of the heap.

3 'Greens', such as lawn mowings.

4 A layer of soaked and chopped straw.

5 'Greens' mixed with coarser waste go into the bin next.

6 Now more soaked and chopped straw.

7 'Greens' mixed with 'browns'.

8 Torn or shredded newspaper.

9 Keep going until the compost bin is full, to create a 'hot' heap. Or, add waste a bit at a time, to give you a 'cold' heap, which takes longer to break down.

Compost

What is it? Anything that was once alive can be composted – even woolly jumpers – but for all practical purposes, it's mainly vegetable matter that goes into a compost bin. There are also a few items that can't be used for compost (see page 16).

When you garden organically, the idea is that you feed the soil, which then feeds the plants, rather than giving the plants artificial fertilisers directly. One of the best medium-fertility soil conditioners of all is garden compost. Not only does it add some nutrients, it is also ideal for opening up heavy clay soils, and for making free-draining, sandy soils more moisture-retentive.

You can buy compost – organic ideally – for improving the soil (different from the sort you use for sowing seeds) at any garden centre. Or even better, make compost yourself. It's free and this also means you are doing your bit for the environment by recycling green waste rather than adding to landfill sites.

The compost bin

You can simply make a compost heap, but there is no doubt that a bin is more practical, particularly in small gardens. It speeds up the composting process and it looks neater. There are a number of different types of bin that you can make or buy, but they all need to fulfil the basic criteria:

- They need an open base, to allow worms to enter from the soil to speed up decomposition.
- They need solid sides, to keep in the heat generated by the process of decomposition, and a lid or cover, which will hold the heat in, as well as keep the rain out.
- The bin should be easy to fill and it should be easy to get at the compost, both to turn it during the process to incorporate the air that's essential for decomposition, and to use it when it's finished.

For a very small garden, a worm bin is ideal, but for a larger garden, it is worth making your own compost bin(s). For Delia's kitchen garden we made a pair of adjoining square, wooden bins, known as New Zealand bins, each 1m x 1m x 1m (3ft 3in x 3ft 3in x 3 ft 3in), with sliding planks at the front for ease of access. The idea of having two bins is that when you're making the compost the contents of the first bin can be tossed into the second – a good way of incorporating more air once the original supply has been used up. When the first batch is ready, you can start making the second.

Recipe for compost

The secret of successful compost-making is to get the balance of ingredients right. You need some moisture, some nitrogen and some air and, if you have the right mix of raw materials, you will have all three naturally without needing to add any extra.

What to put in a compost bin

1 Soft waste – 'greens'

These, being mainly leafy, will give you nitrogen and water and are quick to break down. They include:

Lawn mowings These must be mixed in with coarser waste otherwise, they can form a slimy, smelly mass

Small, soft weeds These should be leaves only – do not put in roots, seeds or bulbils (small bulbs)

2 Coarser waste

This also contains nitrogen and water, but its firmer structure helps to keep the compost 'open', allowing air in. It takes longer to break down and comes from:

Plant waste From ornamental plants, discarded bulb foliage, soft hedge trimmings, and so on

Waste from the vegetable garden Top growth of peas and beans, outside lettuce leaves, carrot tops, etc

Fruit and vegetable kitchen waste Lettuce leaves, tea bags, tea leaves, coffee grounds, vegetable peelings

Cut flowers Once past their best

3 'Browns'

These are also coarse waste – they contain nitrogen and water, but they are firmer still and are slow to break down. Shred 'browns' to speed up the process a bit, or at least chop them up with a spade. The materials vary and, confusingly, browns (such as discarded leaves) can sometimes be green.

Chopped-up or shredded prunings Make sure they are thin and not too woody

Tougher discarded leaves Cabbage, Brussels sprouts, other brassica stems, etc

Paper Shredded or torn-up newspaper, cardboard tubes, papier mâché egg boxes

Straw Chopped-up or dampened straw, or discarded straw bedding from pet gerbils, hamsters, rabbits

Also Egg shells, bigger, tougher weeds, discarded old annuals, stems of herbaceous plants

Sow forth

1 Use a line to make sure the rows you sow are straight.

2 Tip a small pile of seeds into the palm of your hand.

3 Take a small pinch and sprinkle the seeds very thinly along the watered drill.

4 Fill in the drill with dry soil.

5 Sow large seeds individually along the drill.

6 Push some seeds, such as squash or beans, into the soil when sowing.

7 When sowing crops that are not very reliable when it comes to germinating, station-sow in clusters of two or three seeds at each station.

8 Always label the rows clearly.

What not to put in a compost bin

Any waste meat or fish products This is because they can attract rats

Diseased plant material Brassicas with club root, rose leaves infected with black spot, onions with white rot

Any underground parts of perennial weeds Docks, nettles, oxalis, for example

Annual weeds carrying masses of seeds Although, if the compost really heats up, they will be killed, there's always a chance that some will survive

Persistent perennial weeds Bindweed or ground elder

Plastic or metal These materials will not break down

Hot or cold compost?

If you can fill a bin rightaway, you will get results much quicker because the contents heat up and decompose much more easily. This is called a 'hot' heap. 'Cold' heaps, where the waste is added a bit at a time, don't reach such high temperatures, and so take longer – though the end product is just as good.

For most of us with smaller gardens, filling the bin in one go is not realistic, but even so, it is better to add as thick a layer at a time as you can – 10-15cm (4-6in) is ideal. So store the

different types of waste by the bin until you have enough collected to make a reasonable layer.

To get you started, you could even ask your non-composting neighbours for their lawn mowings or the local greengrocer for some of his waste fruit and vegetables.

Green manure crop

Another way of fertilising the soil is to sow a green manure crop. This is a crop that is grown to be dug into the soil as a fertiliser before the next crops are sown or planted – making it a good substitute for compost.

During the winter, green manure is particularly useful on light soils because it helps to stabilise them and also lock in nutrients that would otherwise be washed away by the winter rain. When dug into the soil in the spring, the chopped-up foliage provides a good source of nitrogen.

There are a number of varieties of green manure for sowing in spring and summer, but in autumn, the best bets are phacelia, vetches and Hungarian grazing rye.

The latter two contain compounds than can inhibit germination, so use them only where you are going to plant out seedlings or sets in the spring, not where you plan to sow seed directly into the soil. Or, you can dig them in at least one month before you plan to sow.

Go green Use green manure like compost, to fertilise the soil before crops are sown or planted

Sowing

Sowing seeds outside

The first step to sowing any seeds is to make rows of shallow drills (straight grooves) in the soil – you want evenly spaced, straight rows. It saves time if you mark a bamboo cane or wooden batten, using a permanent marker, with spacings – 2.5cm, 5cm, 10cm, 15cm, 30cm (1in, 2in, 4in, 6in, 12in). Then it's very easy to measure the distance between rows (and between large seeds and young plants later on, when you need to set them out).

To ensure your rows are dead straight, always use a line. You can buy a garden line or make a simple one with two stakes and some brightly coloured twine – the length of your longest row. The kitchen garden will not only look better but all your crops will be at the optimum spacing.

Using the line as your guide, make shallow drills 5mm-1cm (¼-½in) deep with the corner of a hoe or even of a spade. If the soil is dry, water along the drill carefully, using a watering can, and wait until the excess has drained away. Then sow the seeds.

Always be very mean with seeds when you are sowing them. When they germinate, you have to thin them out, so sowing meanly now means less thinning out and less waste later.

Never sow seeds directly from the packet – that almost inevitably means you will spill them and end up with dozens if not hundreds of seeds in one spot! Instead, tip a small pile of seeds into the palm of your left hand (if you are right-handed; the other way round if you are left-handed). You may see some experts sowing the seed directly from the side of their hand, but again, as a novice

gardener, you are more than likely to wind up with some very uneven sowing if you do it that way.

The best method for fine seeds is to take a small pinch of them with your right (or left) hand and sprinkle them as thinly as possible along the drill. If you have any seeds left in your hand at the end, put them back in the packet. Don't be tempted to go back over the drill with the remainder. You will just undo all your good work! With medium-size seeds, such as spring onions, radishes or spinach, you can space them individually 1cm (½in) or so apart.

However, with larger crops, such as cabbages, where you will need at least 15-23cm (6-9in) between plants, you'll need to sow seeds at greater distances apart. Also, some vegetables are not reliable when it comes to germinating and you have to build in a margin for error by sowing in clusters (two or three seeds at each station). This is known as station sowing. If they all come up, you simply remove the weaker seedlings. When you have sown your seeds, fill in with dry soil. You don't need to water again immediately. The seed will have enough moisture in the drill from the watering before sowing and enough warmth from the dry soil to start germination.

Another way to sow seed is by the wallpaper paste method – suitable for slow-germinating crops such as carrots, parsnips and onions. About 10 days before you plan to sow, sprinkle some seed thinly on to wet kitchen paper in the bottom of a plastic food box. Keep it somewhere warm – at about 21°C (70°F) – and, after a few days, the seeds will start to sprout. When the bulk of the seeds have sprouted, mix up some wallpaper paste (it must be without added fungicide) at half the strength given on the packet. When it has

Starting seeds off

1 Tipping multipurpose compost into seed trays.

2 Another option is to use pots.

3 Biodegradable pots break down in the soil, ensuring no root disturbance when planted out.

4 You can also sow in Jiffy 7s, hard discs of dried compost.

5 You need to soak the Jiffy 7 first so that it swells to form a pot.

6 Sowing a single seed in a Jiffy 7.

thickened, carefully wash the seeds off the kitchen paper into a fine mesh nylon sieve and then carefully stir them into the paste. Pour the mixture into a plastic freezer bag and tie a knot at the top. Make a drill 2cm (¾in) deep, snip off one corner of the bag and carefully pipe the mixture along the drill. Fill in with soil and cover with two layers of fleece. These seedlings should emerge between two and three weeks earlier than seed sown in the usual way.

Look out for seed tape too. This is a strip of biodegradable paper with individual seeds already spaced about 5mm (¼in) apart. Cut the length of tape you want – a full or part-row – and just lay it in the bottom of a 2cm (¾in) deep drill, before filling in with soil.

Many times, you will only need to sow part-rows – you don't want 10 lettuces all ready at the same time! As soon as the first seedlings are through, sow another part-row. Remember to mark each row with a label on which you have written the name of the variety sown (and the date if you like).

If you have space, you can sow seeds outside in a seed bed before transferring seedlings into their final position. If not, sow inside and plant out the seedlings.

Module display
Above left Seeds sown separately in modules
Above right Modules in the heated propagator

Sowing seeds inside

The technique for sowing inside is the same for all seeds. The reason you sow inside is to get ahead, as crops will germinate more quickly, especially with the bottom heat that is provided by a heated propagator. It doesn't have to be fancy. The cheapest and most basic will do the job very well. Since the seeds need to be in there for only a few days on average, it gives you as much capacity as you need.

You can sow, using seed or multipurpose compost, in seed trays, pots or plastic modules, or biodegradable pots (which break down completely in the soil), or in Jiffy 7s (small, dried discs of compost surrounded by fine netting, which swell up when soaked in water to form individual planting pots – perfect for larger seeds).

If you sow in seed trays or pots, once the seedlings are through, you will need to prick them out. This means carefully lifting each seedling, taking great care not to touch the roots, and re-planting it in an individual pot. If pricking out sounds a bit fiddly, go for one of the other methods.

Modules are plastic trays of small, individual cells. To sow in these, fill the tray of modules with seed compost, firming it down lightly with your fingers. Then make a shallow depression in the centre of each module with your finger and sow two or three seeds into it. If they all germinate, you remove all but the strongest seedling. Lightly cover the seeds with sieved compost or vermiculite (an extremely lightweight mineral, available from the garden centre), and level it off with a straight edge – a ruler perhaps. It's a good idea to label each row as you go. If you leave this until the end, you might forget which variety is where. Sow biodegradable pots in the same way.

It's broadly similar with Jiffy 7s. Once the disc has been soaked and swollen to form an individual planting pot, make a shallow depression in the centre and sow in that. Draw a little of the moist compost over the top to cover the seed and leave it to germinate. Again, you want a long season of harvesting, rather than a glut, so only sow a few at a time – some now and some more after a week or two.

Watering from the bottom rather than from the top means you won't dislodge the seeds, so stand seed trays, pots and modules in a tray of water. Once the compost is thoroughly moist – it will

Sowing kits

Top left Seedlings coming through in modules

Top right These are sown in pots

Below left Neat rows in a seed tray

Below right Single seedlings in Jiffy 7s

Thinning tactics
Far right Thinning
outside – discarding all
but the strongest
seedlings

Right The remaining
seedlings now have
enough space, water
and nutrients to develop
into healthy plants

be very dark brown and glistening on the surface – leave them to drain for a few minutes and then put them in a heated propagator. If the plants are developing in modules, when it's time for them to go into the garden, all you do is carefully remove each plant complete with its root system in a plug of compost by pushing up from the base. This causes no disturbance to the roots and no set-back in the plant's development.

Biodegradable pots and Jiffy 7s are, if anything, even better, because you simply plant the whole lot – pot and all – so there is no chance of even the slightest disturbance to the rootball.

Thinning

One of the hardest things for new gardeners to do is to thin out seedlings – discarding some so that each remaining one has enough space, water and nutrients to develop into a sturdy, healthy plant. You will be so thrilled that the seeds have germinated that you won't want to throw any of them away, but you must if you are to have healthy, vigorous plants. It is wasteful but there is only a limited amount of water and nutrients, and, if you have too many

plants in competition for them, they will be weak and spindly and much more susceptible to diseases.

Outside, if the soil is dry, water the seedlings an hour or so before you start to thin. It makes the job easier, and helps the survivors recover from the shock more quickly. Ideally, thin in stages, leaving each seedling just clear of its neighbours each time, until they are spaced about 5–7.5cm (2-3in) apart for baby leaf crops. If you want to let them grow on to full-size plants, thin out every other plant in a week or so. Choose the strongest looking seedling – not necessarily the tallest – in each group, and then carefully remove the rest. One way is to place your index and middle finger on the soil on either side of the seedlings and press down, while with the other hand you carefully tease the unwanted seedlings out. This saves disturbing the roots of the one that remains.

Another method is to use an old table fork to loosen the soil around each group. Remove the unwanted seedlings, then immediately firm the soil around the remaining one. If there is a big gap in the row, lever out a small clump of seedlings with plenty of soil around the roots and use it to fill the gap. The same principles

Gentle persuasion
Far left Using a dibber to ease a seedling out, taking care not to disturb those that are left

Left Thinning aubergine seedlings to leave one per biodegradable pot

apply to thinning seedlings sown inside in trays, Jiffy 7s or biodegradable pots. But when thinning seedlings sown in trays, remove the seedlings you want to keep and pot up individually.

Hardening off

Plants sown in the greenhouse usually need to be hardened off before being planted outside. This means acclimatising them to the colder conditions outside the greenhouse by putting them in a cold frame with the lid opened a little wider each day. If you don't have a cold frame, stand them outside in a sheltered spot (say, in the shelter of a warm wall) for a few hours during the mildest part of the day, around lunchtime, and gradually increase the time until they are out all day and night. Initially, cover the plants with a plastic propagator lid with the vents open, taking it off after a few days. Otherwise, going straight from the warm,

Playing it straight
Above left Planting out, using a line as a marker to keep the row straight as you work
Above right A good, strong root system

still conditions inside to cooler, windier ones will be too big a shock. The leaves may shrivel a bit if the wind is cold and cropping can be delayed. If you're planting out under a cloche or fleece, the plants don't need to be as fully hardened off.

Planting out

Once the seedlings have been hardened off, they are ready to go out into the garden. Give them a good watering an hour or so before you plant them out to lessen the shock of being transplanted and help them recover quickly. If necessary, lightly dig over the soil, so that it's loose and level it with a rake or even the back of a fork. Use a line to make sure the rows are straight and, if you don't trust yourself to judge short distances apart by eye, use a bamboo cane or wooden batten marked with various distances (see page 17) laid alongside the row. Make a planting hole

Pest control

Far right Protective collars fit snugly around brassica seedlings to ward off cabbage root fly

Right In an effort to deter carrot fly, stronger smelling onions are planted alongside carrots

deep enough to take the seedling or the biodegradable pot or Jiffy 7, and put it in, then gently firm the soil around it. With some crops, such as courgettes and pumpkins, plant more deeply with the stem buried up to the seed leaves. Once they are planted, give them all another good watering to settle the soil around them.

When planting seedlings into containers, we used machine-made terracotta pots for crops such as aubergines, peppers and chillies because they are not expensive and you can take off some of the rawness of the colour by painting them with some very dilute white emulsion – about 1 tbsp to ½ litre (¾ pint) of water – to simulate the limed look that old terracotta has.

Diseases, pests and crop protection

You'd be a very lucky kitchen gardener indeed to come through a whole season without encountering any problems at all with pests and diseases. There are whole books devoted to the subject and various useful websites (see page 165), so what is dealt with here are the most common pests you are likely to come across most often and suggested ways of dealing with them. Since

we were growing produce to eat, we decided early on to use no chemicals at all in Delia's kitchen garden but to garden organically. Put very simply, one guiding principle of organic pest and disease control is to grow strong and healthy plants, and grow them 'hard' by not being over-generous with fertilisers. That way you do not encourage the very soft, sappy growth that pests love.

Another important technique is attracting creatures that eat pests into the vegetable plot. Provide shelter for toads, frogs and hedgehogs, which eat slugs, and give shelter and food to birds, which will eat slugs, snails and eggs, as well as caterpillars. In among the vegetables, sow open-faced, pollen-rich flowers to attract beneficial insects such as ladybirds, hoverflies, and their larvae, which feast on aphids.

Some gardeners swear by companion planting – disguising the smell of one vulnerable crop by planting a stronger-smelling one alongside it – onions to deter carrot fly is a good example of this practice, or savory to keep the aphids off broad beans.

Finally, there are various mechanical or barrier methods of protection that can be very successful in keeping pests at bay.

Slugs and snails

A slug eats twice its body weight in foliage every day so it's not surprising that they can demolish a row of seedlings overnight and turn cabbage or lettuce leaves into lace. One way to defeat them is to sink traps into the ground. These can be purpose-made, or use old cream or yoghurt cartons, filled with beer. Attracted by the smell, the slugs and snails fall in and drown. Or, surround young seedlings with something sharp in texture over which slugs and snails won't crawl – baked, crushed egg shells, sharp grit, or minerals sold for this purpose. To protect larger seedlings, such as brassicas or runner beans, use a large plastic bottle with the top and bottom cut off to act as a mini cloche. Push it into the soil around the plant. Not only will it keep the slugs and snails off, but it will create a beneficial micro-climate around the plant to boost growth.

Ground beetles will eat small slugs and snails (along with caterpillars, leatherjackets and eelworms among others). They feed at night, so provide somewhere cool and damp for them to hide in the day – a few slates or flat stones. You could also lay planks in the vegetable garden at night, under which slugs and snails will gather after feeding. Then turn it over in the day, so that birds can eat them.

If slugs are more of a problem than snails, try a biological control – nematodes (microscopic multicellular animals), which are watered on to the soil once it has warmed up and attack slugs underground. They don't harm other creatures and don't affect crops.

Flying pests

The easiest method of protecting vulnerable crops such as brassicas, peas, and certain root crops from flying pests (cabbage white butterfly, pea moth, carrot fly, cabbage root fly) is to erect a simple protective cage, using enviromesh. This allows light and water in but keeps the pests out. You can buy these cages ready-made or make your own with plastic ball joints, dowelling or bamboo canes and mesh, weighted down around the beds with stones or bricks. To protect against carrot fly, erect a mesh screen about 60cm (2ft) high with no top. Carrot fly are low-flying and, luckily, haven't the brain power to work out that all they need to do is fly up a bit and then down again. They are attracted by the smell of carrots, which is why the less thinning (which releases the smell) you have to do the better.

Protect brassicas from cabbage root fly with a collar that fits snugly around the stem of the plant and prevents the female from laying her eggs. You can buy these ready-made or make your own from carpet underlay. To do this, cut out 15cm (6in) squares, then make a slit from the middle of one side to the centre, where you also cut a small 'X'. Fit this snugly round the stem of the plant.

Aphids

These small insects come in a range of colours – green, black, white, pink – and attack a variety of plants, sucking the sap, and sometimes transmitting viruses in the process. Eternal vigilance is the best method of defence. As soon as you spot aphids, squirt them off with a hand sprayer (a dash of washing-up liquid in the water helps) or squash them between your thumb and finger. They breed very quickly – females can breed at a week old – but if you act at the first sign, you can prevent an infestation. Ladybirds, lacewings and hoverflies, and especially their larvae, can eat huge amounts of aphids, so, to attract them, plant flowers such as dwarf convolvulus, pot marigolds and field poppies – with your vegetables. Broad beans are particularly vulnerable to blackfly. Planting in autumn helps, as does pinching out the soft, sappy growing tips in May.

Pesticides

If you find you can't keep pests under control without pesticides, there are organic ones available. If possible, choose those that kill only the pests and not the beneficial insects, and remember that 'natural' does not automatically mean 'safe'. If you spray with derris (a natural insecticide) for example, wait at least 24 hours before harvesting the crop, and don't use it near a pond as it is toxic to fish. If you use non-organic pesticides, do so as a last resort and spray only in the evenings when most of the beneficial insects are no longer flying. Check carefully on the label to see how long after spraying you can safely harvest. If you must use slug pellets, use them sparingly and, if possible, hide them under a piece of slate or a tile so that other creatures don't eat them.

Friends and foes
Above left The larvae of ladybirds can eat a vast amount of aphids, so plant flowers to attract them
Above right Set traps or scatter grit to ward off snails

PROTECTING THE CROPS

Cover story

1 A bell cloche, which is useful for small kitchen gardens.

2 A simple enviromesh cage is another idea.

3 A modern tent cloche made of polypropylene panels set at an angle and clipped at the top.

4-9 Making a polythene tunnel cloche, using dowelling and alkathene water piping to make the frame for a UV stabilised plastic cover.

Cloches

Crops need protecting from pests but also against the cold and to encourage an earlier start to cropping. There is a whole range of options to suit all tastes and budgets. The square, leaded-glass, Victorian-style lantern cloches are elegant but expensive. Glass or plastic bell cloches are good for individual plants, while tent cloches are good for rows. These are flat panels – traditionally made of glass, but these days, usually of double-skinned polypropylene, which is obviously much safer – set at an angle just like a tent and clipped together at the top.

The tent cloches we used in Delia's garden had special long wire supports that ran down the ribs of the panels on either side and into the soil for stability. Another way of protecting several rows of crops at the same time is with a polythene tunnel cloche made from coated tubular steel hoops over which you stretch a fitted zip-on cover made from clear UV stabilised plastic. This is an ideal way to cover growing crops because it allows maximum light in, and the zips make it very easy to gain access to the plants.

If you are on a tight budget, you could always make your own tunnel cloches. The late gardening expert Geoff Hamilton made his with lengths of alkathene water piping for the hoops with short bamboo canes or dowelling inserted at either end to push into the soil. They were fixed in place with a short nail, which was also used, once the polythene was stretched over, to secure the ends of a piece of twine over the outside to keep the polythene in place. In his really budget-conscious mode, Geoff used the polythene that dry cleaning came wrapped in, but that is flimsy these days, so you are better off using a stouter kind. At either end, bunch the polythene together and either weight it down with a brick or bury it in the soil.

Perhaps the easiest option, although it doesn't offer quite as much protection for plants as some of the other methods, is the floating cloche. This is basically a piece of horticultural fleece (available from any garden centre), which is laid loosely over the plants and held down round the edges with bricks or stones.

Crop rotation

While there are some permanent plants in Delia's kitchen garden – the fruit trees, the rhubarb and the asparagus bed – the crops in the other beds will change on a three-year cycle. So where potatoes and courgettes grew in the first season, beans and peas will grow in the next. The potatoes and courgettes will move into the beds where we grew brassicas and root crops, while they move into the beds occupied by the beans and peas. Crops, such as salad leaves and other catch crops (lettuces, radishes, spring onions or spinach), or sweetcorn, can go anywhere there is room.

This is called crop rotation and there are several reasons for doing it. Firstly, if you grow the same crops in the same soil year on year, there is likely to be a build-up of pests and diseases that attack those crops and your yields will suffer. Secondly, different crops make different demands on the soil and, by rotating them in the right order, you use the nutrients most efficiently. Potatoes and courgettes, for example, are greedy feeders, so the soil needs plenty of well-rotted manure and compost added before planting – two heaped spadefuls of compost or one heaped spadeful of manure to 1sq m (10.8sq ft).

Some traditional gardeners say you should manure the ground in the autumn. Organic gardeners believe that if you do this most of the nutrients will be washed out of the soil by the winter rains before you sow or plant crops. There will be enough nutrients left in the soil for most of the beans and peas after the potatoes and courgettes have been harvested, although runner beans, themselves greedy feeders, will benefit from an enriched planting trench (see page 30). Peas and beans – the legumes – have nodules on their roots that fix nitrogen in the soil, and, since that's the element which boosts leaf growth, leafy crops benefit from following the legumes.

Year one

Potatoes/courgettes/pumpkin

Brassicas and leafy greens/Bulbs, roots and stems

Beans and peas

Year three

Brassicas and leafy greens/Bulbs, roots and stems

Beans and peas

Potatoes/courgettes/pumpkins

Year two

Beans and peas

Potatoes/courgettes/pumpkin

Brassicas and leafy greens/Bulbs, roots and stems

Key elements

Above left A rose with a fine spray is essential

Above right Early in the morning is the time for watering the onion bed

Watering

When to water?

In dry weather, you need to water regularly but how regularly depends on the time of year. Obviously, when the weather is cold, you need to water far less often. In hot, dry, windy weather you'll need to do so virtually every two days if not every day.

During periods of wet weather, you don't need to worry at all, but beware the light shower. You may think that it has rained but, especially after a dry spell, it will have barely moistened the surface of the soil, so you will still need to water.

The most effective time of day to water is in the early morning, with evening a close second. Watering during the evening has disadvantages, mainly because some crops – basil is a prime suspect – are more prone to diseases such as mildew if they go through the night damp. Also, damp soil at night encourages kitchen garden enemies number one – slugs and snails.

How to water?

It is more efficient to water the soil rather than the leaves because then the water goes straight down to the roots where it is most needed. It is true that some water is absorbed through the leaves, but generally, they form a canopy over the soil.

A constant flow
Above left Watering along a drill outside
Above right Giving tomatoes a soak in the greenhouse

How much water?

'Water well', the books say, but what does that mean? On a warm, sunny day, 1sq m (10.8sq ft) of crops will lose over 5 litres (over 1 gallon) of water, so that is the minimum amount you need to replace and most experts reckon you should apply twice that amount – 10 litres (about 2.2 gallons) per square metre. Even on a cool, cloudy day, over 1 litre (2 pints) will be lost. (If it's easier to think in terms of length, rather than area, 10 litres will water a row 4m (13ft) long and 25.5cm (10in) wide.) Many watering cans hold 2 gallons of water so it's easy to measure the water you are applying. If you want to use a hose, time how long it takes to fill a 2-gallon watering can with the hose. Counting is more practical than timing with a watch, since it's easier to count in your head each time you water than it is to check your watch. Then you'll know that's how long it takes to apply 10 litres (2.2. gallons) to each square metre.

Which water?

Rain water is best for plants, so do think about a water butt by the house or the garage. If you have a water meter, it will also save you money! Delia's greenhouse has an underground tank built in, with a hand pump, which we used for watering the greenhouse plants, but an external water butt is easily fitted to any down pipe. You can even find square water butts now, which fit neatly against the wall and take up less space than the traditional, round kind.

If you are growing plants in a greenhouse, it's always a good idea to leave a full watering can in there overnight. That means that when you come to do the watering in the morning, the water will be at the same temperature as the compost and so it won't come as such an unpleasant shock to the plants' roots.

Automatic watering

If you're away a lot, think about an automatic watering system, with a water computer, which you attach to the tap, then programme to come on once or twice a day and for however long you like. You could use a sprinkler, or there are DIY systems, with narrow pipes, plugged into a special hose, with sprayers or drippers on the end. These are ideal in greenhouses where all the crops are in containers.

Some useful gardening terms

annual a plant with a life cycle of one year.

bare-rooted plants, such as raspberry canes, which are sold when dormant with no soil around the roots.

biodegradable pots planting pots made of natural materials that break down completely in the soil.

blanching excluding light to make leaves and stems more tender.

bolting crops that flower and run to seed prematurely.

catch crops fast-maturing crops, such as radishes, sown between slower-growing crops.

chitting leaving seed potatoes in a light, frost-free spot to develop short, sturdy shoots before planting.

companion planting types of vegetables grown together acts as a deterrent to pests. Growing strong-smelling onions with carrots deters carrot fly, for instance.

compost soil conditioner mainly made from vegetable matter.

cordon fruit trees with a single central stem, usually grown at 45°. You can also get single, double or triple cordons of soft fruit such as redcurrants.

crop rotation the practice of planting different crops each year in the same beds in a sequence over, say, three years, to get the most out of the soil and avoid the build-up of pests.

crown the part of plants, such as asparagus and rhubarb, from which the growth develops.

cut-and-come-again crops quick-growing plants that are picked as individual leaves rather than harvested whole.

drills shallow, straight grooves made in a prepared seedbed.

earthing up with potatoes, this means, drawing soil from spaces between rows, creating ridges. This gives a greater depth of soil in which the plant can produce tubers, thereby increasing the crop. The greater depth also helps prevent the tubers from turning green and becoming inedible. With trench celery, or leeks, earthing up is a means of blanching the stems. Using a length of plastic pipe for celery does the same job without making the celery muddy.

espalier a tree with a vertical main stem and pairs of horizontal branches trained flat on either side of the main stem.

enviromesh fine mesh sheet used for pest control.

fan fruit trees, trained flat in the shape of a fan.

germination when the seed produces leaves.

green manure specially grown crops that are dug into the soil to add nutrients.

hardening off moving young plants from the greenhouse outside for a period each day to accustom them to cooler temperatures before planting out.

Jiffy 7s small discs of dried compost that form single planting pots.

lifting the practice of lifting vegetables, such as potatoes, at the end of the cropping season to eat straightaway or store.

maincrop potatoes that crop later than earlies and provide tubers that can be stored over the winter.

modules plastic seed trays with individual cells.

mulch a thick layer of compost, manure, bark, etc, spread over soil to keep moisture in and weeds out.

part-rows short or part-rows of fast-growing catch crops, planted a few weeks apart, to avoid a glut.

perennial a plant that dies down in the winter but produces new growth every spring.

pinching out removing the tips of main shoots to encourage side shoots.

planting out transplanting seedlings developed in the greenhouse to the outside garden.

pollination pollen from male flowers used to fertilise female flowers and produce fruit.

pricking out carefully removing individual seedlings from a seed tray and planting them singly in a pot.

propagator plastic trays with lids that speed up germination.

ridging up rather like earthing up, this is done to support asparagus once it has turned to fern to stop wind rock and damage to the crowns.

seed trays plastic trays used for sowing seeds.

self-blanching crop this doesn't need earthing up while growing.

sets small bulbs of onions and shallots sometimes heat-treated to prevent bolting, Quicker than seed.

sow placing seeds, mainly in soil or compost, to germinate.

standard a tree or shrub with a clear single stem and a head of branches at the top, often pruned into a ball.

station sow sowing small clusters of seeds at intervals, which increases the chances of germination with some crops.

thinning carefully removing surplus seedlings, leaving more light, water and nutrients for those left to develop into strong plants.

true leaves these are the second and subsequent pairs of leaves, which appear after the seed leaves that first emerge at germination.

truss a group of flowers that develops into fruit on plants.

tuber the name for swollen underground stems such as potatoes.

Spring

March

The days are getting longer, the soil is beginning to warm up – it's the ideal time for sowing

TASKS FOR MARCH

Chit seed potatoes

Plant herbs, onions

Prepare runner-bean trench

Protect peas

Sow broad beans, Brussels sprouts,
calabrese, carrots, cauliflowers, celery,
herbs, leeks, lettuces, peas, radishes, rocket,
spinach, spring onions, sprouting broccoli,
sweet peas, turnips

Train fruit trees

If you are starting now, as we were in Delia's kitchen garden, you can still grow almost any crop you like this season. At the back of the book, there is a list of the varieties we grew (see page 164).

In the garden

Beans and peas

Broad beans Being so large, these seeds are very easy to sow individually. Sow them 7.5cm (3in) deep, 23cm (9in) apart and in single rows 45cm (18in) apart or sow double, staggered rows in a trench 23cm (9in) wide. To prolong the cropping season, sow in succession – make a second sowing when the first seedlings are 5cm (2in) high. It's worth sowing a couple of spares at the end of each row, just in case one or two don't germinate, so you can replace them later.

Peas These don't germinate in cold, wet soil so, if the conditions aren't right, wait until the soil dries out and warms up a bit towards the end of the month. Make a flat-bottomed trench, 15cm (6in) wide and 5cm (2in) deep. Sow the peas 5cm (2in) apart in two rows 10cm (4in) apart. The space between drills depends on the final height of the peas you are planting. Feltham First is a dwarf variety, reaching only 45cm (18in), whereas Delikett is taller (102cm/40in). So, if you are planting both varieties, leave 45cm (18in) between the rows of Feltham First, and more for Delikett. Cover carefully with soil so you don't dislodge the peas.

Mice love pea seeds, so, if they are a problem in your garden, cover the drills with fine chicken wire, pushed well down into the soil on either side and at the ends, to keep the vermin out. As soon as the peas germinate, remove the wire. In a cold garden, cover the bed with horticultural fleece weighted down with stones or bricks. This will warm the soil up a little, while letting air and water through. It will keep cats off, too. Or, you can start germinating the peas in plastic guttering in the greenhouse (see page 35).

Runner beans Dig a trench for the runner beans, about a spade's width and a spade's depth. These beans are very greedy feeders and one way to ensure they have plenty of nutrients is to start filling the trench now with kitchen waste, such as fruit and vegetable peelings. (The ideal time to start the trench is in the autumn, see page 116, but, if you are starting your garden now, it's still worth doing.) Cover each layer very lightly with soil and when you plant out the beans in two months' time it will be breaking down into good organic matter.

Brassicas and leafy greens

Spinach This is a fast-maturing crop, especially if you eat it as baby leaves. For the latter, sow very thinly in drills 1 - 2cm (½ - ¾in) deep. If you want mature spinach, bear in mind that the final spacing for the plants is 15cm (6in), so either sow thinly and use the thinnings later as baby leaves or station sow – three or four seeds 15cm (6in) apart and remove all but the strongest seedlings if they all germinate. Rows should be 30cm (12in) apart, but if you are growing the spinach in a brassica bed, make the rows 45cm (18in) apart to allow for a row of slow-maturing brassicas in between.

Bulbs, roots and stems

Asparagus Order one-year-old asparagus crowns now for delivery at the beginning of next month. The recommended variety Theilim F1, is an all-male asparagus, which has the advantage of cropping more heavily and not seeding itself as female varieties do. If you can't find an all-male kind in the garden centre, you can buy it by mail order.

Carrots It is especially important to sow carrot seed very meanly as its main pest, carrot fly – the larvae of which burrow into the carrot – is attracted by the smell released when the plants are disturbed. So, the less thinning out you need to do later, the better.

Sow part-rows, about 45cm (18in) long, and in drills 1cm (½in) deep and 30cm (12in) apart. Sow in succession, making a second sowing when the first seedlings are through. Alternatively, use seed tape (see page 18).

Onions While you can grow them from seed, it is easier and quicker to grow onions from sets – very small bulbs that are often heat-treated to prevent them from bolting (running to seed). Make a drill 2cm (¾in) deep and, depending on how large you want the onions to grow, space the sets 5-10cm (2-4in) apart. Don't forget that smaller onions might be more useful if there's only one or two of you. Cover them with soil so that the neck is just showing above the surface. If there are long tufts of skin sticking up, trim them with a sharp knife or scissors because the birds love pulling them out. If

Off to a good start
Far left Sowing pea seeds in a flat-bottomed trench outside, in two rows 5cm (2in) apart

Left Plant red or brown onions in a drill 2cm (¾in) deep and space them 5-10cm (2-4in) apart. Cover with soil so the necks just show above the surface

they do, don't push the sets back down again because you will damage the root plate at the bottom of the bulb. Instead, dig them up carefully and re-plant. If birds have been a menace, bury the set completely. The onions will take longer to mature – that's all.

Growing onions with carrots is an example of companion planting, an organic method of pest control. The smell of the onions is said to disguise the smell of the carrots and so confound the carrot fly. Tests, however, have shown that for this to be truly effective you need a huge quantity of onions per row of carrots. But certainly, planting them in alternate rows can do no harm. In cold gardens, cover the bed with horticultural fleece to keep the frost off it and to stop the birds from trying to pull up the onion sets. Once the sets are planted, you can leave them to grow and develop, ready for summer.

Radishes and spring onions These are very fast-maturing crops and it is sensible to grow them in the same bed as brassicas because radishes take between four to six weeks from sowing to harvesting and spring onions take six to 10 weeks, whereas brassicas take several months. So you can produce a couple of crops of radishes and spring onions long before the brassicas take up the space. To avoid gluts, sow part-rows – 30-45cm (12-18in) – of radishes and spring onions now, and then another part-row in

DELIA IN THE KITCHEN Spinach

Very green and very good for you, spinach is packed with vitamin C. What you need to be most aware of is that spinach contains a great deal of water, so what looks like a huge amount won't be when it's cooked.

Fresh spinach can be rather dusty or muddy. The best way to deal with this is to pick out and discard any damaged or brown leaves and remove any tough stalks, fill the sink with cold water, then plunge the spinach in the water and swirl the leaves around. Do this in two or three changes of water, then let it all drain in a colander, shaking it well over the sink. Young spinach leaves can be wiped and used raw in a delicious salad. If you're serving spinach as a vegetable you will need 225g (8oz) per person, see the cooking method on page 51 ∎

a couple of weeks' time, or when the first sowing has come through.

Sow both radishes and spring onions very thinly in drills 1cm (½in) deep. Make the rows 30cm (12in) apart to allow for the brassicas to be planted out between them in a few weeks. If you are simply growing radishes or spring onions on their own, the rows need only be half that distance apart.

Turnips Sow the seed thinly, a part-row at a time.

Salad leaves

Lettuces This is an ideal catch crop and can be grown anywhere there's room. It is also the great glut crop – a dozen lettuces all ready at once, half of them bolting before you can eat them. So only sow a short part-row each time – 50cm (20in) maximum – in drills 1 - 2cm (½ - ¾in) deep. This allows for three mature hearting lettuces, after thinning the seedlings to 20cm (8in) apart – so sow very thinly indeed. To get off to a flying start, you can also sow some lettuces inside (see page 35).

Rocket Sow a part-row of rocket outside now in drills 1cm (½in) deep. Wild rocket is more peppery but the leaves are thinner and tougher than some of the cultivated varieties.

Soft-fruit bushes

Blackcurrants, gooseberries, raspberries, redcurrants If you are planning to buy container-grown soft-fruit bushes by mail order, order them now to plant next month.

Fruit trees

Apricots, figs, peaches The walls of a kitchen garden are the perfect spot for trained fruit trees. The walls offer protection to the trees and also, they provide additional warmth – the bricks act like storage heaters, absorbing the warmth in the day and then slowly letting it out at night, so keeping the temperature a few degrees higher and therefore reducing the risk of any frost damage to the blossom.

Trained fruit trees grown flat against walls or fences are available as cordons – single stems grown at 45°; espaliers – a central stem with pairs of arms growing horizontally on either side; or fans – as the name suggests, six or so branches spread out in a fan shape.

While it is possible to buy 'maiden' trees – single, untrained stems – if you are a beginner it's certainly best to buy two or three-year-old trees with the training already underway. Unlike vegetables, fruit trees are a permanent feature in the garden and will last for many, many years.

In Delia's kitchen garden, there are apricots, *Prunus* 'Moor Park' and *Prunus* 'NL Early', peaches 'Duke of York' and 'Peregrine' and a fig, *Ficus carica* 'Brown Turkey', all fan-trained (see opposite). Although these were bought as two-year-old trees with the training well underway, more was needed, so horizontal wires were fixed to the walls behind the trees, two courses of bricks apart. Metal vine eyes were used – fixed by drilling holes in the mortar, pushing in wall plugs and then screwing in the vine eyes.

To protect the bark from chafing, do not tie the branches directly on to the wires. Tie each branch to a bamboo cane and then tie the cane to the wire. Use soft but strong twine doubled, and tied in a figure of eight, making sure that the point where it crosses over is between the branch and the cane, forming a cushion. Once the branch is attached to the cane, attach the cane to the wire, using the same method, pulling each branch down slightly, where necessary, to create an evenly spaced fan.

Herbs

No kitchen garden is complete without herbs, and in Delia's kitchen garden, we had four small beds in the centre and several herb pots. These are the herbs we grew.

Grown from seed: basil, chervil, coriander, curly parsley, flat-leaf parsley

Bought as plants: chives, mint, rosemary, sage (green and purple), tarragon, thyme

Some herbs – basil, coriander and chervil – are annuals, which means they last only a season – and, while parsley is technically a biennial with a two-year life cycle, it is probably best to grow it as an annual.

Others herbs are perennial, which means they go on year after year. Some, such as chives, mint and tarragon, die down in the winter but come back again in spring. Others are evergreen – rosemary, sage and thyme. You can grow all of them from seed, but it's easier to buy perennials and evergreens as plants.

There are lots of varieties, varying in size, rate of growth, colour of flowers and leaves (purple sage tastes just as good as green), and, of course, flavour. With tarragon, for example, always go with French not the much less well-flavoured and coarser-textured Russian variety. Experiment and you'll soon find your favourites.

Training session

Top left In Delia's garden an apricot tree is trained into a fan shape. First, fix wires to the wall behind the tree, using metal vine eyes

Top right Attach the branch to the cane, securing with twine

Below left The next stage is to use twine to attach the cane to the wire

Below right The full fan effect is achieved. The mellow brick wall makes the perfect backdrop for it

Fit to burst Seed potatoes ready to be chitted: Pink Fir Apple, Desirée and International Kidney

Coriander, chervil, chives, mint, rosemary, sage, tarragon, thyme In early spring, you can sow hardy annuals such as coriander (make sure it's a variety recommended for leaf rather than seed) and chervil directly into the soil in drills 25.5cm (10in) apart. Sow thinly and, once the seedlings appear in two to three weeks, depending on the temperature, thin in stages until the plants are 15cm (6in) apart. Sow a part–row now and another when the seedlings appear, to keep a succession going through the summer.

Plant chives, mint, rosemary, sage, tarragon and thyme directly in the garden or in pots. Mint will take over if not restrained. Plant it in a bucket with the bottom cut out, but check the bucket is 7.5-10cm (3-4in) proud of the soil or the mint will spread along the ground, rooting as it goes. Otherwise, grow it in a large pot.

In the greenhouse
Beans and peas
Peas To get a head start with either variety of pea (see page 30), especially if you have cold, wet soil or a major problem with mice, sow them in a length of plastic guttering. You can buy this from a builders' merchant. Ideally, it should be cut (using a hacksaw) to the length of the bed into which the peas will be going, and fitted with snap-on ends, which will stop the compost from spilling out.

Fill the guttering with multipurpose compost and water it carefully so that it is evenly moist, but not sodden. For each variety, sow two staggered rows of peas, 5cm (2in) apart. Make sure the compost doesn't dry out both before and after the peas have germinated.

Brassicas and leafy greens
Brussels sprouts Sow seeds now in modules, trays or Jiffy 7s, so you'll have sprouts for Christmas and the rest of the winter.

Cabbages Start varieties of spring and summer cabbages and red cabbage. Spring cabbage will double up as 'spring greens'.

Calabrese This does not transplant well in warm weather, so sow seeds as early as possible in the month to get the seedlings hardened off and planted out next month.

Cauliflowers Sow summer varieties in trays, modules or Jiffy 7s, ready to plant out in April.

Sprouting broccoli This is a slower-growing brassica. Sow it in trays, modules or Jiffy 7s, to harvest early next spring.

Bulbs, roots and stems
Celery Sow either in modules or seed trays and put them in a heated propagator until the seeds have germinated. As soon as they are large enough to handle, thin to one per module or prick out seedlings grown in trays into individual, biodegradable pots.

Leeks Sow leeks in seed trays or in modules thinly and 2.5cm (1in) deep to plant out in May.

Potatoes New and maincrop potatoes are grown from certified virus-free seed potatoes but they need to be chitted before they are planted out next month. Chitting means leaving them in a light, frost-free place to develop short, stocky shoots, 1-2cm (½–¾in) long, which takes about five weeks. You can use papier mâché egg trays. Check which end of the potato has the most eyes – these are where the shoots develop from – then place in the egg tray, so the end with most eyes is uppermost. Or pack the potatoes into seed trays so they hold each other upright.

Salad leaves
Lettuces To start off lettuces inside, you can sow them in trays, and prick them out later into individual pots or modules, or you can sow them straight into modules. They can be planted out at the end of March or the beginning of April and will be ready to harvest a couple of weeks earlier than those sown directly outside.

Herbs
Parsley You can try sowing parsley outside but it is notoriously slow to germinate so, start it off inside in modules.

Flowers
Sweet peas Grow these with runner beans – they look good and attract beneficial insects. They can go out with the beans in May. Sow in pots or modules or, ideally, in root trainers – extra-long modules designed to encourage long roots, which are hinged, so it's easy to remove the seedlings without hurting the roots. Push two seeds into each trainer 5cm (2in) deep. If both germinate, take out the weaker. Otherwise, sow six or so seeds in a 9cm (3½in) pot.

Sow sweet
Holding sweet pea seeds in one hand, sow individually into the compost

March

Chinese Stir-fried Prawns
with Purple Sprouting Broccoli and Cashews

Serves 2

Purple sprouting broccoli responds really well to
stir-frying and in this Chinese-inspired recipe it is perfect – slightly
crunchy and toasted at the edges.

18 raw, shelled tiger prawns (about 225g/8oz)

200g (7oz) purple sprouting broccoli

50g (2oz) unsalted cashews, halved

1 tablespoon cornflour

a good pinch of cayenne

2 tablespoons Japanese soy sauce

2 tablespoons groundnut or other flavourless oil

1 fat garlic clove, chopped

1 dessertspoon grated fresh root ginger

50g (2oz) shiitake mushroom caps
(weight after removing the stalks), thickly sliced

½ teaspoon salt

4 tablespoons rice wine

2 spring onions, cut into 2.5cm (1in) shreds
(including the green parts)

You will also need a large frying pan or a wok, with a lid.

Begin by mixing the cornflour and cayenne in a bowl and
mix well, then toss the prawns into the bowl, and mix, using your
hands, until all the prawns are well coated.

Next, sprinkle in the soy sauce and mix again until they've all
been coated with that, too. Then cover the bowl and leave in a cool
place for about 30 minutes.

Now, prepare the broccoli. Slice the broccoli stalks thinly
on the diagonal, about 5mm (¼in) thick and 2.5cm (1in) in length,
and separate the florets.

After that, heat 1 tablespoon of the oil in the pan or wok over
a high heat. When it's really hot, add the cashews and stir-fry for
30 seconds or until golden, then remove them to a plate.

Now add the prawns and stir-fry for about 2 minutes,
keeping them on the move and tossing them about all the time until
they turn pink. Then remove them to the plate too and keep warm.

Next, add the remaining oil to the pan, along with the
garlic and ginger. Let it cook for 30 seconds, then add the broccoli,
mushrooms and salt – and stir-fry these, again tossing them all
around over a high heat for about 1 minute. Now return
the prawns and nuts to the pan, turn the heat down to medium,
pour in the rice wine and 2 tablespoons water and sprinkle half
the spring onions in. Then put a lid on the pan and cook for a
further minute. Serve absolutely straightaway with the rest of
the spring onions sprinkled over. Either plain or boiled rice
would be a good accompaniment.

Bubble and Squeak Rösti

Serves 4 (makes 8 rösti)

Bubble and squeak is a classic leftover recipe for greens, but making it rösti-style adds a new dimension. These little individual rösti are brilliant served with sausages or leftover cold turkey and ham and a selection of pickles.

450g (1lb) Desirée or Romano potatoes
75g (3oz) spring greens or green cabbage
(trimmed weight)
50g (2oz) mature Cheddar,
coarsely grated
1 tablespoon plain flour
25g (1oz) butter
1 dessertspoon olive oil
salt and freshly milled black pepper

You will also need a baking tray,
25.5 x 35cm (10 x 14in).

First, scrub the potatoes, then place them in a medium saucepan with a little salt. Pour boiling water over to just cover them, then simmer gently with a lid on for 8 minutes.

Drain the potatoes, then, while they are cooling, remove any stalks from the spring greens or cabbage and finely shred the leaves into 5mm (¼in) slices. This is easy if you form them into a roll and then slice them. Drop the leaves of the spring greens or cabbage into boiling water for 2 minutes only, then drain and dry well.

When the potatoes have cooled, peel them, then, using the coarse side of a grater, grate them into a bowl. Season with salt and freshly milled black pepper, then add the grated cheese and greens or cabbage and, using 2 forks, lightly toss together.

To assemble the rösti, shape the mixture into rounds 7.5cm (3in) wide and 1cm (½in) thick. Press them firmly together to form little cakes and dust lightly with the flour.

If you want to make the rösti ahead, place them on a plate, cover with clingfilm – they will happily sit in the fridge for up to 6 hours.

To cook the rösti, pre-heat the oven to gas mark 7, 220°C (425°F), placing the baking tray on the top shelf of the oven. Melt the butter and add the oil, then brush the rösti on both sides with the mixture.

When the oven is up to heat, place the rösti on the baking tray and return it to the top shelf of the oven for 15 minutes, then turn the rösti over and cook them for a further 10 minutes.

Broccoli with Chilli and Sesame Dressing

Serves 3-4

This is something a little different to ring the changes while we have an abundance of broccoli. I think it goes very well with most oriental dishes or just by itself with some steamed rice.

350g (12oz) broccoli
salt

For the dressing
1 teaspoon sesame seeds
1 dessertspoon sesame oil
1 dessertspoon lime juice
1 dessertspoon Japanese soy sauce
1 teaspoon Thai fish sauce
1 small red chilli, deseeded
and finely chopped

First, prepare the broccoli by cutting it into even-sized pieces – stalks and all. Then place a saucepan fitted with a fan steamer on the heat, add the broccoli and pour in about 2.5cm (1in) of boiling water, then sprinkle with salt. Put a lid on and time it for about 4 minutes.

Meanwhile, to make the dressing, you need first of all to toast the sesame seeds. To do this, use a small, solid frying pan, pre-heat it over a medium heat without oil, then add the seeds and toast them, moving them around in the pan to brown them evenly. As soon as they begin to splutter, pop and turn golden, they're ready, which will take about 1-2 minutes.

Then just remove them to a serving bowl and simply stir in all the rest of the ingredients.

When it's cooked, remove the broccoli from the steamer and transfer it to the bowl. Toss everything together and serve straightaway.

April

With a mix of sunshine and typical spring showers, seedlings are off to a good start

TASKS FOR APRIL

Dig trench for celery

Harvest radishes, rocket

Keep adding waste to the runner-bean trench

Plant asparagus, Brussels sprouts, cabbages, calabrese, cauliflowers, chillies, lettuces, parsley, peas, potatoes, soft-fruit bushes, sprouting broccoli, sweet peppers

Protect brassicas, carrots, peas

Put up fruit cage

Sow aubergines, basil, beetroot, borlotti beans, Brussels sprouts, cabbages, cauliflowers, chillies, dwarf French beans, flowers, parsnips, radishes, rocket, runner beans, spring onions, sweet peppers, tomatoes

Begin planting out brassicas and root vegetables this month. Get strawberries planted in pots outside and sow flower seeds. In the greenhouse, start off beans, brassicas and fruiting vegetables. And harvest and enjoy the first crunchy radishes and perhaps some peppery rocket leaves.

In the garden

Beans and peas

Broad beans These should be through now and a few centimetres high. Fill any obvious gaps in the row with spares sown for this purpose.

Peas If peas were sown in guttering in the greenhouse last month, they will now be sturdy little seedlings, ready to go outside, after being hardened off. Water them well before you start, to make them slide out of the guttering more easily. Dig a trench the same width and depth as the guttering, and then remove one of the snap-on ends. You will need another pair of hands to hold up one end of the guttering on the far side of the bed at an angle of about 30°, while you guide the open end into the trench and gently encourage the peas and compost to slide out. It may all come out in one piece but, if it doesn't, guide it into the trench in sections and pat the seedlings down firmly. Give them all a good watering once they are in, just to settle them again completely. Towards the end of the month, when these plants are about 10cm (4in) tall, put in some twiggy pea sticks. These are usually prunings of hazel or birch (although you could use anything else twiggy) and need to be about 45cm (18in) tall or more for the taller varieties. Push the cut ends into the soil at roughly 30cm (12in) intervals but, as the idea is to form a continuous framework for the peas to scramble up, adjust the distance according to the width of the pea sticks. Peas sown directly into the soil won't be as tall as those started in the greenhouse but it won't do any harm to put in some twiggy pea sticks, ready for them to grow up.

Although it's a little early for pea moth, other caterpillars and birds such as jays and pigeons love the

Planting out peas

Top left Watering the pea plants that were sown in plastic guttering last month to germinate

Top right Holding the guttering at an angle, guide the peas into the trench – you'll need an extra pair of hands to do this

Below left Pat the soil down firmly around the peas

Below right Towards the end of April, put in some twiggy pea sticks to support the plants

Bulbs, roots and stems

Asparagus As this is one of the very few permanent crops in the vegetable garden, it is absolutely essential to prepare the soil well, removing every trace of weeds and especially all the perennial weed roots that you possibly can. When you see the spidery roots of the year-old crowns you will be planting, you can understand how they will quite quickly form a tangled mass below the soil. So, if there are any weeds left in the bed, it will be impossible to remove them and they will start competing with the asparagus for nutrients and water and the crop will suffer. Asparagus needs good drainage, so if you have heavy clay soil, you would be better growing it in a raised bed, with plenty of fine grit added. It is a greedy crop, so add well-rotted manure or garden compost at the usual ratio, two spadefuls of compost or one of manure to 1sq m (10.8sq ft) of soil.

It's important to plant the crowns as soon as possible after they arrive and not to let them dry out in the meantime. If yours look dry, put them in a bucket of water for an hour or two, then plant them rightaway. If that's not possible, wrap them in damp sacking.

Dig a trench about 25.5cm (10in) deep and 30cm (12in) wide, then make a ridge of soil just under 15cm (6in) high along the centre of the trench. Handling with care, take a crown and place it on top of the ridge, spreading the roots out on either side. Leave 30cm (12in) between the crowns and 30cm (12in) between rows. Fill in carefully with soil, making sure there are no air pockets around the roots (or they may dry out), until the crown is covered by about 5cm (2in) of soil. As the spears start to push through, in a few weeks, keep adding soil, leaving about 10cm (4in) of spear clear.

Beetroot This is one of the few crops that is salt-tolerant, so it is good for seaside gardens. Beetroot doesn't like the cold. The seed doesn't germinate if the soil temperature is below 7°C (45°F), and exposing the young seedlings to temperatures of below 10°C (50°F) makes them likely to bolt later on. Choosing a bolt-resistant variety such as Boltardy helps, as does covering the bed with horticultural fleece after sowing to raise the soil temperature. For small, golf-ball-size beets, sow in rows 15cm (6in) apart. For larger beets, make the rows 25.5cm (10in) apart. Either station sow – two or three seeds every 7.5-10cm (3-4in) apart, depending on how large you want the beets to grow – or sow very thinly and, once the seedlings are through, thin them to that distance apart.

Carrots If the earliest sowings are large enough to handle,

Starting asparagus

Top left The spidery roots of the asparagus crowns arrive ready for planting

Top centre If your crowns seem dry, soak them in a bucket of water before planting them

Top right Or, wrap them in damp sacking until ready to plant

Above left The trench with a ridge of soil along the centre

Above centre Place crowns on top of the ridge with roots draped on either side

Above right Spears pushing up through the ridges of soil a few weeks later

tender green leaves and shoots, so cover with an enviromesh cage.

Runner beans Keep on adding kitchen waste to the runner-bean trench, if you dug one last month. Cover with a thin layer of soil.

Brassicas and leafy greens

Brussels sprouts, cabbages, calabrese, cauliflowers, sprouting broccoli The brassicas sown in March in the greenhouse can be hardened off, once seedlings appear, then planted out in succession at the end of the month or beginning of next. If you have sown catch crops (fast-growing radishes, spring onions and spinach) far enough apart, there will be room to allow the slower-growing brassicas to go in among them. The cabbages need to be well spaced since they grow to be quite large. To defeat the main pest – cabbage root fly – place collars on each plant to fit snugly around the stem and prevent the female from laying eggs in the soil right next to it.

It is worth planting all the brassicas in one area, as they will need similar protection. To fend off egg-laying butterflies (their caterpillars can soon make lace curtains of brassica leaves) and other pests, make an enviromesh cage for the brassica bed.

Spinach The leaves will be showing soon, and the spinach will be ready to pick as baby leaves in May.

thin them now to about 4cm (1½in) apart and sow another part-row. At this time of year you need to watch out for carrot fly maggots, which will make tunnels in the carrots. It's best to thin your seedlings during the evening, rather than in full sunlight during the day, when the flies are about and can be attracted by the smell of crushed carrot leaves. Protect the bed with horticultural fleece or an enviromesh cage.

Celery Although the celery won't go out until the end of May, dig a trench now, about 30cm (12in) deep and 45cm (18in) wide, and work plenty of well-rotted organic matter into the bottom. If you plan to grow a self-blanching variety (a variety bred not to need earthing up), fill the trench in completely, ready for planting. If you are growing a trench variety, such as Giant Red, fill the trench to within 7.5-10cm (3-4in) from the top, leaving the excess soil for earthing up later. A self-blanching variety is less trouble but not so well flavoured.

Onions These should be starting to shoot now. In unusually dry weather, make sure the soil stays moist.

Parsnips Parsnips don't like the cold so there is not much point in sowing them earlier than this. Either sow very thinly in a row, or station sow, with four or five seeds per station, because parsnips are a bit erratic and the germination rate is not very high. They are also very slow to germinate – it can take up to five weeks. To help you remember where they are when you're weeding, sow a quick-growing crop such as radishes among them. They will mark the row and will be harvested before the parsnips need the space.

Potatoes It's important that the soil is neither too cold nor too wet when the new potatoes go in, otherwise they will not burst into growth and there's a chance that the tubers will rot. If the weather has been reasonably warm and dry for a couple of weeks the soil should be fine, but if it is very wet to touch and feels very cold, wait a week or so to plant. The traditional day for planting new potatoes is Good Friday, which can vary by three weeks, so you can see the timing is not crucial!

To prepare the soil, work in some well-rotted manure and compost – potatoes are greedy feeders, though two spadefuls of compost, or one of manure, is enough for 1sq m (10.8sq ft) of soil.

Dig trenches between 10cm and 15cm (4in and 6in) deep and wide enough to take a seed potato. Space new potato tubers about 30cm (12in) apart – and maincrop varieties 40cm (16in) apart. Allow at least 40cm (16in) between the rows of new potatoes

(earlies) and 65cm (25in) between rows of maincrop. The time potatoes take to grow depends largely on weather conditions. A frost that blackens the foliage in late April or even early May, for example, will delay cropping. The earlies are faster growing and you should be able to harvest them from June, whereas the larger, maincrop potatoes need to be in the ground for much longer – harvested from August – so they need more space to develop.

When planting, stand the chitted potato tubers on end, with most of the shoots facing upwards. Sometimes you find there is an equal number of shoots at both ends, in which case take your pick. Then cover the tubers with soil, taking care not to disturb them.

Radishes and spring onions Carry on sowing part-rows of these. Towards the middle or end of the month, the radishes sown last month will be ready for harvesting. Earlier sowings take much longer to mature than late ones because the soil is not as warm.

To harvest, pull the largest radishes carefully out of the soil, so smaller ones nearby can grow on for harvesting in a few days' time. If you aren't sure how to tell if they're ready, gently scrape away the soil around the base of one of the largest clumps of leaves to see the top of the radish. Often the top will be above the soil anyway, so it's easy to see. If it's a bit smaller than a marble, it's ready to harvest. It's better to err on the side of pulling radishes a bit too small, rather than a bit too big, since the latter become quite dry and woody.

Turnips To make sure you get a decent-size root, thin the seedlings to their final distance as soon as possible – about 10cm (4in) apart for baby turnips and 15cm (6in) for larger ones.

Fast growers
Above left Pull out the largest carefully, leaving the smaller radishes to grow and crop later

Above right A new crop of radishes, ready for springtime salads

All set for soft fruit
ar right Once the
truts of the fruit cage
re assembled, a net
an be stretched over
. Result? Light and
water can get through
ut birds can't

Right Clusters of fruit
buds gleaming among
he leaves of the
edcurrant bush

Salad leaves

Lettuces Seedlings sown in the greenhouse last month can be planted out now. Space them about 15cm (6in) apart. Plant a few lettuces now, followed by a further few in a week's time, to stagger the cropping.

Rocket Sow another part-row. By the end of the month, you may be able to start picking earlier sowings.

I make no secret of the fact that this is one of my favourite salad leaves. Why? It's traditionally English and has been used in salads since Elizabethan times. It has a lovely concentrated buttery flavour and goes with any dressing. Not, I think, good as a salad leaf just on its own, because it's not crisp, and a lot of it seems somehow to be too concentrated and 'in your face'. However, added 50:50 to crisp lettuce, it makes, I think, one of the nicest green salads of all ■

Fruit cage

The one drawback to growing soft-fruit bushes is the fact that the birds enjoy the fruit as much as you do. The answer is to put up a fruit cage that allows light and water to penetrate but keeps the feathery felons out! The cages come in kit form (available by mail order) and they consist of struts that form a framework that is covered by netting. These come in a range of sizes, but always go for the largest you can accommodate. There's nothing more frustrating than putting up a fruit cage, then wishing it were longer!

There was no room in Delia's main kitchen garden for soft fruit, apart from the blueberries and strawberries we grew in pots, so we put up a fruit cage just outside it on a spare piece of open ground that gets the sun all day. It's 7.3m (24ft) long and 5.4m (18ft) wide with a mesh door for ease of access, and it really wasn't difficult to erect.

It's easier to plant the fruit bushes before you put the net on the cage because this gives you more room to manoeuvre. When you are ready, it's simple enough to put the net on with an extra pair of hands and there are clips provided in the kit to secure it to the framework, as well as pegs to fix it to the ground.

Prepare the soil well before planting container-grown fruit as soft fruit is a permanent crop (lasting 10-15 years or so). It likes fertile, moisture-retentive but not boggy soil, so if yours is very free-draining, add plenty of bulky organic matter – composted bark or straw (from the garden centre), or garden compost – to hold the water longer. If it's heavy clay, work in some coarse grit as well as bulky organic matter to open it up and improve drainage. If the structure of the soil is about right, boost fertility with two spadefuls of compost or one of manure to 1sq m (10.8sq ft) of soil.

Soft-fruit bushes

When planting soft-fruit bushes, it's a good idea to mulch well with compost or well-rotted manure between the rows and to lay MyPex (woven matting that lets the water through) to keep the weeds down.

Blackcurrants Whether you are planting container-grown blackcurrants in spring or bare-rooted ones in autumn or winter (see page 129), always make sure you buy two-year-old plants that are certified disease-free. (It's only two-year-old plants that can be certified.) Since you want plenty of new growth to appear from below ground level, it's important to plant both container-grown plants (and bare-rooted) 5cm (2in) deeper than the soil marks on the stems (they show the depth the plants were grown at in the nursery).

Ben Connan blackcurrants have been bred in Scotland to be resistant to frost and to diseases such as blackcurrant gall midge and American gooseberry mildew. While not as compact as Ben Sarek, which is the best variety for very small gardens, Ben Connan is more compact than most and produces large berries with an excellent flavour early in the season.

Gooseberries In Delia's garden, container-grown plants were planted 1.2-1.5m (4-5ft) apart in generous planting holes in soil that had already been dug over and improved with compost and manure. It's important that they are planted at the same level as they were in their pots – the soil mark on the stem is a useful guide.

The object with gooseberry bushes is to create a goblet-shaped plant with an open centre, so prune out any branches that cross in the middle. This is to encourage free circulation of air and help prevent American gooseberry mildew, although the variety we chose, Invicta, has good resistance to mildew anyway. Aim to leave about five main outward-facing

For a row of raspberries
Top left Double wires tied to posts act as support for two rows of fruit canes
Top right Threading wire through stout metal eyes
Above left Preparing the trench
Above right Plant to the soil mark on the stems

branches. Make sure that the bush has a clear stem or leg of about 15cm (6in) above soil level. Gooseberries need plenty of water, especially after they are planted, and also when the fruits are swelling. Then they need around 35 litres per sq m (8 gallons per 10.8sq ft).

These bushes can also be trained as espaliers, single, double or triple cordons, and even as standards – which is a good idea in small gardens where space is at a premium. You can buy them part-trained from specialist nurseries, or you can train them yourself from one-year-old plants.

Raspberries These can be grown in several ways. Where space is at a premium, you could grow three or four canes twisted around a central post. Or, you can grow them in rows, tied to single or double wires. We opted for the latter.

We chose two container-grown varieties (Glen Lyon, a summer-fruiting raspberry, and Autumn Bliss, which fruits from mid-August onwards). We used two stout (10 x 10cm/4 x 4in thick and 2.4m/8ft high) posts, which we stained a soft mossy green with a wood stain – not essential but it looks more attractive. The posts were hammered into the ground 4.8m (16ft) apart and 75cm (2ft 5in) deep, leaving about 1.6m (5ft 2in) of each post above the ground. It is important to hammer them in that deeply because they must be able to support the weight of the fully grown canes and the crop. Next, two cross-pieces 30cm (12in) long were nailed horizontally on to each upright, the first about 1m (3ft 3in) above the ground, the other at the top. Stout metal eyes were screwed into the ends of each cross-piece and 3mm (⅛in) gauge wire threaded through and pulled taut, forming two pairs of parallel wires, one above the other.

We planted the raspberries in a trench deep enough so that the canes were at the same level as they had been when growing in the nursery. This ensures plenty of healthy new growth from below soil level. There will be a soil mark on each raspberry cane, so it is easy to get the level just right.

We planted Glen Lyon about

45cm (18in) apart, and the more vigorous Autumn Bliss raspberries, about 51cm (20in) apart. Summer-fruiting raspberries produce fruit on one-year-old canes, so the growth made during the first summer will produce next summer's fruit. To ensure strong plants for the future, pick off the flowers the first summer. Autumn-fruiting raspberries planted in the spring will produce fruit, although only a small crop in the first year.

Container-grown raspberry canes bought in the spring have been cut down the previous winter by the nursery, so the growth on them is the new season's growth and can stay. This isn't the case with bare-rooted canes planted in the autumn or winter, which need to be cut down to 30cm (12in) after planting (see page 129).

The raspberries need to be well watered after planting. MyPex laid between the rows will suppress the weeds as well as spawn – small raspberry shoots that are not wanted for cropping – which would otherwise deprive the canes of moisture and nutrients.

Redcurrants These are similar to gooseberries, not blackcurrants, in their needs, though it's even more important to ensure they have good drainage as they really dislike waterlogging. We grew our container-grown redcurrants as bushes but you can grow them trained against a wall or fence where space is tight. Red Lake is an old variety which has plenty of long strigs (bunches) of currants, while Rovado is a newer variety with longer strigs of large, well-flavoured berries in August.

Soft fruit in pots

Blueberries This fruit, which has been growing rapidly in popularity in the last few years, does very well in pots – just as well, as it needs an acid soil, which many gardens cannot provide. We decided to grow four bushes in ericaceous (lime-free) compost in large, bulbous terracotta pots and stand them either side of the two side gates of Delia's kitchen garden. We chose two varieties, Blue Crop and Goldtraub. Planting more than one bush improves pollination and therefore gives you a heavier crop.

Strawberries We grew these in terracotta pots along the front of the greenhouse. Not only do they look very attractive, but it is much harder for the slugs to get at them in the pots than when they are growing in the soil, and very easy to net them against birds once the crop ripens. Late summer/early autumn is the traditional time to plant strawberries, but, thanks to a new technique by which the young plants are frozen, you can buy them by mail order (see page 165) any time between late March and July, then plant them for a crop the same year, which is ideal.

We ordered five different varieties, all highly recommended for flavour, cropping at slightly different times. Elvira – an early variety, fruiting from mid June to early July; Gariguette, also an early, and sold in the markets of Provence and London's ritziest food halls; Hapil and Florence, which are both highly prized for flavour and produce fruit through July; Mara des Bois, which has the distinct flavour of wild, woodland strawberries but from normal-size berries – this crops from mid August into September.

Unwrap the plants when they arrive and plant them in groups of four or six in 25.5cm (10in) pots, which are first filled with well-drained compost – a mix of 75% multipurpose compost with 25% fine grit or perlite. The plants will have thawed out by the time you receive them by post, but they very quickly perk up once they're planted. If the weather is unseasonably cold when they arrive, plant them anyway but keep the pots in an unheated greenhouse, conservatory or porch. As soon as the weather is reasonable, they can go outside. If you are growing several varieties, do label them. Although there are differences in the size and colour of the fruit and the leaves, you may not remember which is which, and it's useful to know which variety did best and which had the flavour you preferred.

Herbs

Parsley Plant out parsley if it was sown inside last month.

Flowers

Convolvulus tricolor, cornflowers, love-in-a-mist (Nigella), California and Shirley poppies, pot marigold (Calendula) and the bishop's flower (Ammi majus) In all but the most sheltered, warm gardens this is the best month for sowing hardy annuals. If you sow too early when the ground is cold and wet, the seeds won't germinate until conditions improve anyway and may well rot in the meantime. Sowing from mid April on means a higher success rate with germination, and they grow very quickly. While we had a cutting bed within Delia's vegetable garden, we also sowed annuals in the fruit beds at the ends of the wall (well away from the fruit trees themselves, so that they are not competing for moisture and nutrients) and in some of the other beds where we had room. We chose these varieties because they look lovely and serve

Potting strawberries

Top left A coat of very dilute white emulsion ages machine-made pots (see page 22)

Top right Strawberry plants can be bought frozen, ready for a crop during the same year

Below left Place the young plants in well-drained compost

Below right If the weather is unseasonably cold, keep them inside in an unheated greenhouse, conservatory or porch

Room for growth In the greenhouse various seedlings, including brassicas and root vegetables, are progressing well

an important purpose in the vegetable garden. Their pollen attracts beneficial insects, such as lacewings, hoverflies and ladybirds, which, along with their peculiar-looking larvae, eat huge quantities of pests such as aphids. This is extremely important when you are growing organically and do not want to use chemical pesticides. To sow them, mark out shallow drills – about 5mm (¼in) deep – for each variety, the final spacing distance apart. (It will tell you on the packet what that is.) If the soil is dry, carefully water along each drill before you sow, and let the water drain. Sow extremely thinly. With tiny seeds like those of poppies, this is virtually impossible, but the more sparingly you sow, the less thinning out you'll need to do later. One minute pinch of poppy seeds contains dozens of seeds, while the curious micro shaving brushes that are cornflower seeds are so easy to get hold of you can almost sow them singly. Check on the packet what the final spacing is and allow that distance between rows. Cover drills with dry soil. The mix of moisture below and warm, dry soil on top will get them germinating.

In the greenhouse
Beans and peas
Borlotti beans, dwarf French beans and runner beans
At the end of the month, start these off in Jiffy 7s, modules, pots or trays. For the latter, space the seeds about 7.5cm (3in) apart. For modules and pots, push one seed down into the centre of each hole/pot, so that it has at least 2.5cm (1in) of compost on top of it and make sure that it's covered. If the compost feels dry, water it thoroughly and let it drain completely before you put the beans into the heated propagator.

Check them every day, not that the beans will sprout up like magic, but because the lid will be covered in condensation and if you lift it off, turn it upside down and then tap it sharply, you can direct the water that gathers back on to the compost

The beans should germinate within three to five days. As soon as the shoots appear, take the plants out of the propagator and stand them on the bench.

Brassicas and leafy greens
Brussels sprouts, cabbages and cauliflowers You can sow more sprouts now. Keep on sowing spring and summer cabbages and cauliflowers for late summer and autumn cropping.

On a blue note
Far left The seeds of cornflowers are like tiny shaving brushes

Left The flower seedlings are starting to emerge

Bulbs, roots and stems
Celery and leeks Keep the plants well watered.

Fruiting vegetables
Aubergines Bearing in mind that you will get only a few decent-size fruits from each plant, decide how many you want to grow and indeed have space for. Sow them as you would tomatoes (see below), although they like an even higher temperature to germinate – between 21-30°C (70-86°F).

Chillies and sweet peppers Sow as for tomatoes.

Tomatoes Sow from about the middle of the month. If you are planning to grow tomatoes outside, the plants will be about the right size to go out at the end of next month, when all danger of frost has passed. Decide how many plants of each variety you want – three or four will give you plenty of each type. If you are planning to grow them inside, as we did, you can sow a little earlier.

For each plant, sow two or even three seeds about 1cm (½in) deep per Jiffy 7 or biodegradable pot. If all of them germinate, remove all but the strongest seedling. Alternatively, you can sow all the seeds of one variety in a single pot and when they have germinated, prick the seedlings out into individual pots. The first way means you don't have to move the fragile seedlings and risk any damage. Either way, place them in a heated propagator – even though you are sowing in the protection of a greenhouse, fruiting crops like these need high temperatures to germinate. As soon as the seedlings appear – within three to five days – take them out of the propagator and treat them as you would beans (see left).

Herbs
Basil Start basil plants off from seed in modules or Jiffy 7s.

April

Spinach and Ricotta Soufflés with Anchovy Sauce

Serves 8 as a starter

Having spinach in the garden is a perfect joy. The very young, textured leaves are great in salads and the taller, darker green leaves for cooking. I have collected masses of lovely spinach recipes over the years but have only recently tried this one, which for about 20 years has been one of the signature dishes of Langan's Brasserie, Mayfair, one of my most favourite restaurants in the world. Here, I have set out my own interpretation. As usual with soufflés, everything can be made well in advance and then all that needs to happen is the egg whites get whisked and incorporated just before cooking.

For the soufflés
900g (2lb) spinach leaves
50g (2oz) ricotta cheese
50g (2oz) butter, plus a little extra for greasing
the ramekins
freshly grated Parmesan, for dusting the insides
of the ramekins and sprinkling on top of the soufflés
275ml (10fl oz) milk
50g (2oz) plain flour
4 large eggs, separated

freshly grated nutmeg
a pinch of cayenne
salt and freshly milled black pepper

For the anchovy sauce
1 x 200ml tub crème fraîche
1 tablespoon anchovy essence
or 1½ tablespoons anchovy sauce
a good pinch of cayenne pepper
a squeeze of lemon juice

You will also need eight 4cm (1½in) deep ramekins with a base diameter of 7.5cm (3in), and a large baking sheet.

Pre-heat the oven to gas mark 5, 190°C (375°F), and pop the baking sheet in to pre-heat, too.

First of all, butter the ramekins and lightly dust the insides with Parmesan. Then thoroughly wash the spinach in several changes of cold water and pick it over, removing any thick, tough stalks or damaged leaves.

Next, pack the leaves into a large saucepan, sprinkle in some salt (but don't add water), cover and cook over a medium heat for

4-5 minutes. Just let it collapse down into its own juices and then give it a stir halfway through. Now drain the spinach thoroughly in a colander, pressing it very firmly with a saucer to extract every last bit of juice, it needs to be quite dry. Then chop it fairly finely.

Now pour the milk into a saucepan, then simply add the flour and butter and bring everything gradually up to simmering point, whisking continuously with a balloon whisk, until the sauce has thickened and becomes smooth and glossy.

Then turn the heat down to its lowest possible setting and let the sauce cook very gently for 5 minutes, stirring from time to time. Next, remove the pan from the heat and transfer the sauce to a large bowl.

Now beat the chopped spinach and the ricotta into the sauce with the egg yolks. Then season with salt, pepper, a generous amount of nutmeg and the cayenne. Beat the egg whites in a large, clean bowl till stiff, then using a large metal spoon, fold one spoonful into the spinach sauce to 'loosen' it.

Now carefully fold the remaining egg whites into the spinach mixture before dividing it equally among the 8 ramekins. Sprinkle the tops of the soufflés with a little Parmesan and bake for 25-30 minutes, or until well risen and slightly browned on top.

While the soufflés are cooking you can make the anchovy sauce. Put the crème fraîche into a small saucepan and bring it up to simmering point and cook gently for 5 minutes, then stir in the anchovy essence (or sauce), cayenne and a good squeeze of lemon juice.

The soufflés need to be served hot and puffy from the oven and at Langan's they make an incision into each soufflé with a knife and pour in a little sauce, then hand the rest around separately in a jug.

Crisp Roast Duck
with a Confit of Rhubarb and Ginger
Serves 6

Rhubarb and I go back a long way. Though I've only recently acquired a proper kitchen garden, I've always grown rhubarb in our Suffolk garden – well, actually, it just appears every year and grows all by itself. Dark rosy luscious stalks that have become the staple of crumbles, tarts and fools. Just for a change, this recipe includes it in a savoury dish. Very crisp roast duck with its richness complemented by the acidity of rhubarb.

2 x 1.8kg (4lb) Gressingham ducks
fresh watercress, to garnish
sea salt and freshly milled black pepper

For the rhubarb and ginger confit
500g (1lb 2oz) rhubarb, cut into 2cm (¾in) chunks
1 heaped teaspoon of finely grated fresh ginger
480ml (17fl oz) dry cider
150ml (5fl oz) cider vinegar
125g (4½oz) golden caster sugar

You will also need a large roasting tin, 5 x 25.5 x 35cm (2 x 10 x 14in) and a roasting rack or some kitchen foil.

You need to start this recipe the day before to make sure the ducks are as dry as possible before you cook them. So, prepare them by removing and discarding the wrapping and giblets. Then dry them with a clean tea cloth and leave them, uncovered, on a plate in the fridge till needed.

The next day, pre-heat the oven to gas mark 8, 230°C (450°F) and prepare the ducks by wiping them again. Then, using a small skewer, prick the fatty bits of skin on each duck, particularly between the legs and the breasts. Now, either place the ducks on the roasting rack or make a rack yourself for each one by crumpling some kitchen foil and placing it in the bottom of the roasting tin. Season the ducks generously with sea salt and freshly milled black pepper, using quite a lot of salt, as this encourages crunchiness. Now place the tin on the centre shelf of the pre-heated oven and roast the ducks for 1 hour and 50 minutes. During the cooking time, using an oven glove to protect your hands, remove the tin from the oven and drain the fat from the corner of the tin – do this about three times (the fat is brilliant for roast potatoes so don't throw it away).

Meanwhile, to make the confit, all you do is place all the ingredients in a large saucepan, stir well, then bring everything up to simmering point. After that, turn the heat down to a low setting and let it simmer gently, without a lid, for 45-50 minutes. It's very important not to stir it at any stage as this will break up the pieces of rhubarb and make it mushy. What you want to do is retain some of the shape and texture. It's ready when it is covered with a dark, sticky glaze and there should be no more than about a tablespoon of liquid left at the end. When the cooking time is up, allow the ducks to rest for 20 minutes or so, then carve and serve the duck with the confit and garnished with fresh watercress.

May

Summer's almost here and now warmer, longer days are encouraging healthy new growth

TASKS FOR MAY

Earth up potatoes

Harvest carrots, lettuces, radishes, rocket, spinach, spring onions

Mulch fruit cage

Plant basil, borlotti beans, Brussels sprouts, cabbages, cauliflowers, celery, cucumber, dwarf French beans, leeks, runner beans, tomatoes

Protect beans, peas, strawberries

Put up runner-bean framework

Remove summer-fruiting raspberry flowers

Ridge up asparagus

Sow beans, beetroot, cabbages, carrots, cauliflowers, courgettes, cucumbers, parsnips, pumpkins, rocket, spinach, spring onions, sweetcorn, turnips

Depending on the weather, watering at this productive time is crucial, and different crops have slightly different requirements. So it's not just a question of sticking the sprinkler on for a while and watering the whole plot. (It must be said, though, that using the sprinkler is far better than not watering at all if that is the only option!) Give peas or beans too much water before they start flowering, for example, and they produce leaves rather than flowers. But, after flowering, regular watering will improve the quantity and texture of the crop. It's the same with root crops such as parsnips and carrots – too much water means masses of leaves, but doesn't produce any more roots. But with crops grown for their leaves, obviously, a steady supply of water right the way through the growing season is ideal to promote the production of lush, green leaves.

In the garden

Beans and peas

Borlotti beans and dwarf French beans Borlotti Lingua di Fuoco, a climbing bean can either be grown up canes in rows or up wigwams, as you do with runner beans, planting one bean at the base of each cane (see page 56). All climbing beans climb clockwise, so when you are helping them cling on at the beginning, twine them in that direction. Alternatively, borlotti beans can be grown up a bean and pea netting 'wall' – netting stretched between two strong, tall canes on either side of the row. Plant them early in May.

Towards the end of the month, when all danger of frost is past, plant out the dwarf French beans, having hardened them off for a week or so first. These need no support, unlike climbing beans. Plant them about 23cm (9in) apart, in rows 45cm (18in) apart.

Slugs are a major pest of all young beans – they will vacuum up everything except the toughest bit of main stem – so protect them with a barrier of sharp grit, Organil, an organic product based on crushed eggshell, or cinders spread in a 15cm (6in) circle around the base of each plant. Or, use 20cm (8in) sections

of 2-litre (3½-pint) plastic drinks bottles with the tops and bottoms cut off, placed over each plant and pushed well into the soil. If you must use slug pellets, try to use a type that is safe for other kinds of wildlife and pets.

If you didn't sow beans under cover at the end of April or the beginning of the month, sow them directly into the soil now. Sow three per cane or per station for the non-climbing dwarf French beans, with a view to removing the weakest if they all germinate. As with most crops, sow in succession – half a row now, another half row when these are through – to ensure the longest cropping season. Some people find that soaking beans (and peas) in water for a few hours before sowing speeds up germination.

Broad beans Their soft, juicy tips are a prime target for blackfly. If you don't want to use chemicals, pinch out the growing tips – the top 5-7.5cm (2-3in) – as soon as the first young pods have appeared.

Good for peas
Above left Give peas protection by covering them with a simple enviromesh cage
Above right A healthy crop climbs up the pea sticks

Peas At the beginning of the month, all the early sowings of peas will be flowering, and this is the time to increase the watering to swell the seed pods that are forming as the flowers die. If you haven't protected peas with an enviromesh cage, do so now, and make sure the edges are securely weighted down. The little creamy grub that you sometimes find in pea pods, having munched its way through some of the peas, is the caterpillar of the pea moth. It lays its eggs when the plants are flowering in early summer. The enviromesh keeps them out but allows water and light through.

We learnt the hard way in Delia's garden. The mesh at one corner of the cage was not secured firmly, the wind caught it and left part of the bed unprotected. It took only a day for something to get in and lay its eggs and soon after, we found that many of the leaves were eaten away and caterpillars were still in evidence. We did get a crop

Pole position

1 To make a framework for runner beans, push poles into the soil on either side of the trench.

2 Cross each pair and secure with twine. Carry on until the whole row is up.

3 Place another pole across the 'Vs' and secure it.

4 Plant out the runner beans.

5 Scatter over a layer of Organil, an organic product based on crushed egg shells.

6 Sweet peas in root trainers, ready to be planted alongside the beans.

7 Planting sweet peas next to the poles.

8 Tie firmly to the poles with twine, finishing with a reef knot.

of peas but it was not as generous a crop as we hoped we'd have.

Runner beans Now is the time to stop adding waste to the trench and to cover it with a layer of soil. Put up a framework to support the runners. Use either hazel poles or thick bamboo canes, at least 2.1m (7ft) long and place them in pairs, one on either side of the trench, leaning in towards the centre and about 20cm (8in) apart. Push them well down into the soil – about 30cm (12in) if you can. A good crop of runner beans is very heavy!

Pull each pair of poles or canes together so that they cross about 30cm (12in) from the top, and lash them together with stout twine. When the whole row is up, place another hazel pole or cane horizontally in the 'Vs' formed by the crossing poles and lash them to it. This will provide even more stability. Alternatively, make a wigwam with six, eight or 10 hazel or bamboo canes. Pull them all together at the top and lash them tightly.

At the end of the month, plant out the runner beans in the same way as you'd plant dwarf French beans, after hardening them off. Remember to add some kind of protection against slugs. Add the sweet peas sown in March to the row, tying them to the poles as you plant them to start them climbing. Not only do they look pretty but they also attract valuable pollinating insects.

Incidentally, if you have not got around to digging the runner-bean trench yet (and it happens!), it will pay you to dig it at least 60cm (24in) deep and spread a thick layer of well-rotted manure or garden compost in the bottom of the trench, then cover it over with soil to which you have added a couple of handfuls of pelleted chicken manure per linear metre (3ft 3in). Then leave it to settle for two weeks before planting the beans out.

Brassicas and leafy greens

Brussels sprouts, cabbages and cauliflowers Plant out more brassicas, including cabbages sown in April, with protective collars. It's worth using the collars, even if you have covered the bed with an enviromesh cage – the belt and braces approach! Water the newly planted seedlings well to help them settle fast in their new position.

Spinach If you want to eat your spinach as baby leaves, you should be able to start harvesting now when the leaves are 5-7.5cm (2-3in) long. Pick a few leaves from each plant, rather than picking all from just a few, so the plants will go on producing new leaves. Or, if you cut a whole plant at the base, as opposed to pulling it root and all from the ground, a second crop of leaves will re-grow from the stump.

If you like spinach, sow another short row early in May and one halfway through. Some varieties of spinach, such as Hector F1, are less inclined than others to bolt or suffer in hot weather. Choose one like this for sowing from now, and wait until August to sow other types. Water well to prevent spinach from bolting.

Bulbs, roots and stems

Asparagus By the middle of this month, the trenches you dug for planting last month will be more or less filled in with soil as the spears have started to grow. Still aiming to keep about 10cm (4in) of the stems clear, start ridging up, using the soil between the rows to make ridges around the bases of the spears. This helps prevent the spears and the fern into which they turn later from being rocked by the wind that damages the crown, and also helps

the plants to develop strong, well-anchored root systems. In really windy gardens you might need to stake each one.

Keep the asparagus well watered and free of weeds. A thick (10cm/4in) mulch of well-rotted manure or compost helps to keep the moisture in and prevents annual weeds from germinating.

You really mustn't pick or cut any asparagus in the first year – not even one little spear – because the plants need to build up their strength. In the second year, you can cut one or two spears as a reward for good behaviour, but then leave the plants to put their energies into a strong root system that will result in heavier crops from the third year onwards.

Beetroot Towards the end of the month, when the beets sown in April should be starting to swell, give them a good soaking. It's much better to give them plenty of water and then leave them for a week or so, than to water little and often, as this encourages the growth of leaves at the expense of roots. You can eat the leaves rather like spinach. Sow more beetroot for a continuous harvest – maybe a part-row.

Carrots At the beginning of the month, carry on thinning the carrots sown in March (some of the thinnings may even be big enough to eat in salads). From the middle of the month on, some of the carrots will be ready for harvesting. The smaller the carrots are, the crunchier and tastier they will be. You want them to be about finger size. If you can see the top of the carrot above the ground and it is about

Take root
Above left Young carrot plants are now ready for thinning. Thinnings may be big enough to eat in salads
Above right Planting out celery plants, using a line of twine to keep the row straight

the size of a small coin, it should be right. If you can't see the top, just carefully scrape a little soil away to check. On light soils, you should be able to pull the carrot out. On heavier soils, you may need to loosen the soil around it with a hand fork first. To avoid attracting carrot fly, harvest in the evening and not in bright sunshine.

Water the carrots in dry weather but don't overwater them because that encourages the growth of more leaf than the actual carrot. Try to be consistent with watering – it helps to prevent the carrots from splitting. Sow another part-row to give you plenty for the summer months ahead.

Celery Harden off the plants from the middle of the month, ready to go out at the end. Once they have about five true leaves (as opposed to seed leaves, which are the first pair of leaves that come through when the seed has germinated), you can plant them out – about 30cm (12in) apart, in rows also 30cm (12in) apart. Make sure that the crown of the plant – the point from where all the leaves are growing – is just at soil level. Celery must be kept well watered or it can turn out to be stringy. Water it once or twice a week, depending on the weather.

Leeks When the seedlings are 15-20cm (6-8in) high and looking like skinny spring onions or chubby chives, you can plant them out. Using a dibber, make holes about 15cm (6in) deep and 15cm (6in) apart. Drop a leek into each hole, so that the roots are resting on the bottom, and then fill the hole with water. Don't fill in with soil. Watering will start the process of settling soil around the roots and the holes will gradually fill up. If you don't have space in the beds yet for the leeks, they will wait for another month or two.

Onions Keep free of weeds. Now that they will be growing well, you don't need to water them unless the weather is very dry.

Parsnips If the seeds have germinated successfully, thin to one seedling every 10-13cm (4-5in). If the weather is very dry – no rain for weeks – water them every week or two with 11 litres per sq m (2 gallons to 10.8sq ft). Keep them free of weeds. Another part-row sown now should germinate more quickly and successfully than the earlier sowings as the soil is warmer.

Potatoes The potatoes should be coming on, particularly early cropping varieties, such as International Kidney. The most important job to do now is earthing up, which means that, once the plants are about 23cm (9in) tall, you need to draw soil from the spaces between the rows up around the plants. This will form a series of ridges and valleys in the bed. Depending on how easy your soil is to work, you may need to break it up with a fork first. The reason you do this is to create a greater depth of soil as the plant grows so it can produce more tubers as it does so.

All lettuces and salad leaves should be eaten as fresh as possible, but first of all I've found the best way to store lettuces is to remove the root, but otherwise, leave them whole and enclose them in a polythene bag in the lowest part of the fridge. I believe washing should be avoided if possible, as, once the leaves are wet, it's difficult to dry them again and you simply can't get dressing on to wet salad leaves. What I prefer to do is take a damp piece of kitchen paper and wipe each leaf – this way the lettuce leaves remain dry and can more easily be coated with dressing. Now, I realise many people will not agree with me here and will want to wash the leaves: in that case plunge the separated leaves briefly into cold water and place them in a salad basket, then either hang them up after a good shaking or else swing the basket round and round out of doors. Finish off by drying the leaves carefully with kitchen paper ∎

Earthing up also prevents the tubers situated nearer the surface from being exposed to daylight and turning green, which renders them inedible, indeed poisonous. Aim to leave about 13cm (5in) of top growth exposed, giving the plants enough food-making capacity to ensure healthy growth. Earth up in at least two stages, especially for earlies.

Growing potatoes under black polythene, with 'Xs' cut into it to allow growth through, keeps the light out without the need for earthing up, but it does make watering more fiddly.

Earlies need plenty of water – 15-20 litres per sq m (3-4 gallons to 10.8sq ft) every 10-14 days if there has been little or no rain. Maincrop varieties, on the other hand, do best if they are not watered before marble-size tubers have formed (carefully scrape away a little of the soil at the side of the ridge to check progress, but always replace all the soil to prevent the potatoes from turning green). When those small tubers have formed, water them at the ratio shown before.

Radishes Continue to harvest them as they are ready. Aim to keep the soil moist, but do not overwater, otherwise you encourage leaf at the expense of root.

Spring onions These take a little longer to mature than radishes but you should be able to start harvesting them this month, too. To see if they're ready, look at the size of the bulb – the top of it may well be clear of the soil. If it's not, scrape a little soil away. Pull as many as you need, leaving any undersized ones to grow on for a few more days. To keep them going, sow more part-rows 30-45cm (12-18in) every week to 10 days. Keep them well watered in dry spells.

Turnips Keep them watered and clear of weeds. Sow another part-row at this stage.

Salad leaves

Lettuces Hearting lettuces (as opposed to the loose-leaf or salad-bowl types that never form a heart), such as All The Year Round or Lobjoits, are meant to be harvested whole, rather than as single leaves, and, as soon as they have nice firm hearts, they are ready to pick. It's better to pull up a lettuce first thing in the morning and keep it in the fridge, even if you don't plan on eating it until lunchtime or the evening. That's because there is more moisture and flavour in the leaves at the beginning of the day.

Rocket Keep picking and sowing part-rows. Rocket bolts quickly if you don't keep harvesting. If it does bolt, pull the plant out now and sow some more.

Working with soil
Top Drawing up soil around potatoes gives the tubers more depth of soil in which to grow

Above When spring onions are ready, you can usually see the tops protruding above the soil. If not, scrape soil away gently to check

All about leeks

Top left A tray of spindly leek seedlings

Top right Use a dibber to make holes about 15cm (6in) apart

Below left Lower each leek so that the roots are resting on the bottom of the hole

Below right Fill up the holes with water which will settle the soil around the roots. Don't fill with soil – the hole will gradually fill up anyway

A study in pastels

Top left Cornflower – a glorious shade

Top right Convolvulus – delicate cream and lilac with sunshine yellow centres

Below left Open-faced flowers, such as the poppy, are ideal for attracting beneficial insects

Below right Love-in-a-mist in flower. The more you pick now, the more blooms will be produced

60

Soft-fruit bushes

Keep the soil free of weeds around all the fruit in the fruit cage – a thick mulch and the MyPex should go a long way to doing this for you but hand-weed in any gaps. Raspberries, for example, are very shallow-rooting and so using a hoe can damage them.

Blackcurrants These need a lot of water at each watering – 50 litres per sq m (11 gallons per 10ft 8in). How often you need to water depends on the weather. If it's hot, and especially when the fruit is beginning to swell and turn colour, it's vital that the soil doesn't dry out. Water carefully, and do not splash water on to the lower leaves of the bushes because that can encourage diseases.

Gooseberries Watch out for caterpillars of the gooseberry sawfly. On more established bushes, this is the time to thin out and remove every alternate fruit. You can use the hard green berries that you remove for cooking.

Raspberries It's hard, but in the first season after planting, you should remove all the flowers of summer-fruiting raspberries. This allows all the plants' strength to go into producing a strong, healthy root system that will pay dividends in future years. If that is too much to ask, just leave a few flowers on one or two canes so you'll have at least a taste of the delights to come. In dry weather, keep them well watered, particularly once the fruits on established plants start to form and swell. Make sure you water carefully on to the soil, avoiding the emerging new canes and the fruits, since wetting the foliage can encourage diseases such as botrytis (the fungal disease that causes grey patches to appear on leaves).

Redcurrants Although redcurrants dislike waterlogging, they do need ample water – 25-50 litres per sq m (5.5-11 gallons to 10.8sq ft) – once the fruits start to swell and turn colour.

Soft fruit in pots

Blueberries Make sure the compost doesn't dry out.

Strawberries The main hazard to strawberries in pots is overwatering. In saturated compost, the roots will turn black and die. The first sign that this has happened is when you notice the leaves flagging. You might suspect that they need watering, but always check the compost before you do. If it is already moist, then

don't add more. If it's just one plant in the pot with a problem, remove it because it won't recover. The others may be successful. The best cure is prevention – planting in a mixture of 75% compost and 25% grit or perlite gives the balance of moisture retention and good drainage that strawberries need. In dry weather give the pots a good soak and then let the compost almost dry out before you water them again.

As soon as the strawberries begin to flower, start regular liquid feeding – once a week – until the fruits begin to ripen. Use a fertiliser high in potash, such as tomato fertiliser, according to the rate given on the bottle.

If there is a danger of frost at night, cover any strawberry plants in flower with horticultural fleece. Once fruits begin to form and turn colour, protect from the birds with netting.

Fruit trees

Apricots It's unlikely that you will get much fruit in the first year on new plantings but, from the second year on (particularly on trees that have had the protection of a polythene sheet over the winter, see page 139), by the end of May, you should find plenty of small, green fruits. Apricots don't usually produce as heavy a crop as peaches and thinning out may not be necessary. If it is, leave about 7.5cm (3in) between fruits.

Figs In the first year of planting you won't get lots of fruit but as the tree matures, you'll get plenty more.

Peaches You should see lots of small, furry, green peaches appearing this month – more from the second year onwards after planting. Now comes the hard bit – thinning them out. In order to produce decent-size, lush peaches later in the summer, you really need to leave just one fruit per cluster and thin them still further next month so that they finish up 15-20cm (6-8in) apart. You may find that means removing more than you're keeping but just conjure up the image of a ripe, juicy peach in your mind and do it! If you don't, you'll wind up with small, hard fruits that you won't want to eat. (Incidentally, if you are growing nectarines instead, thin them to 15cm/6in apart.)

Signs of summer
Above left Blueberry flowers are creamy white
Above right As the strawberry flowers fade, the fruits can be seen starting to form

Fruiting well
Above, from left
The small green fruits of the peach tree start to appear. Thin them at this stage

In the greenhouse, aubergines are being thinned to just one plant per pot

Putting the aubergine plant into a pot. They don't need staking as tomatoes do

A sweet pepper plant flourishing

Herbs

Basil The basil that was started inside in April can't go outside until all danger of frost is past in mid to late May.

Flowers

Convolvulus tricolor, cornflowers, love-in-a-mist (Nigella), California and Shirley poppies, pot marigold (Calendula) and the bishop's flower (Ammi majus) These will need thinning out, especially the poppies. This is because poppy seed is so fine that it is impossible to sow it as thinly as most other annuals. Thin to about 5cm (2in) apart and, in a couple of weeks' time, thin to 15-20cm (6–8in), depending on the variety, then water to help the survivors settle down again. As soon as they start producing flowers, which could be as early as at the end of the month, begin to pick them. The more you pick the more they will produce.

In the greenhouse
Brassicas and leafy greens

Cabbages and cauliflowers You can still sow some more of these to plant out for late autumn or winter cropping. Sow a winter variety of red cabbage now, too, to plant out next month.

Fruiting vegetables

Aubergines, chillies and sweet peppers As soon as the seedlings are a decent size – about 2.5cm (1in) high, thin them to just one per pot. Towards the end of the month, plant them in their final (25.5-30cm/10-12in) pots in John Innes No 3 or in a 50:50 mix of John Innes No 3 and multipurpose compost. They will not need staking now in the way that tomatoes do.

Cucumbers At the beginning of the month, sow these in biodegradable pots that are only half filled with compost. (You will see why they are only half full later.)

The seeds are very large but flat so it's best to sow them vertically rather than horizontally. That is because the seed case is still attached to the new leaves as they push through the compost and it's much easier for them to push up the narrow edge, rather than the broad, flat surface.

Once they have germinated – in three or four days – and the seed leaves and any true leaves (as opposed to the fleshy, oval seed leaves) have reached the top of the pot, fill in carefully around the stem with compost to support the stem and encourage strong roots.

About two weeks after sowing, when they have three or four true leaves, they are ready to be planted either outside (in which case you should harden them off for a week or so first) or inside the greenhouse, which is where they were grown in Delia's garden.

We grew cucumbers in growing bags, rather than pots, so support for the plants was needed. One easy way to support them is to attach very strong twine to the roof struts of the greenhouse, and then, when you plant the cucumbers in the growing bag, place the other end of the string in the compost, under the cucumber plant to hold it firmly.

In Delia's greenhouse, the sloping roof was too high for attaching strings, so we put up two brackets on the back wall about

2.2m (7ft) above the growing bags, and threaded wire between them on to which we tied twine. Towards the end of the month, the cucumbers were planted out into the growing bags, with the stem buried up to their seed leaves. This gives them more support and makes for stronger plants.

Tomatoes As soon as the tomato plants are a reasonable size, about 7.5cm (3in) tall (if you planted them in Jiffy 7s, you will just be able to see the roots through the sides), plant them in their final pots – plastic or terracotta pots 25.5-30cm (10-12in) in diameter are fine.

Terracotta pots look more attractive but plastic pots are slightly more practical as water does not evaporate through their sides as it does with terracotta. Use either soil-based John Innes No 3 or a 50:50 mix of that and multipurpose compost.

Before you plant, place a bamboo cane at least 1.2m (4ft) tall in each pot. It is easier to do this now, rather than waiting until the plant needs support, because you don't risk damaging any roots as you push the cane into the compost. As soon as the plants are about 23cm (9in) high, start tying them to the cane. Use soft twine, doubled and tied in a figure of eight, crossing between the stem and the cane. This prevents the stem from chafing against the cane and possibly allowing diseases in.

As the tomatoes grow, you'll see side shoots appearing where the leaf stems join the main stem. Snap these out with your finger and thumb – you'll find they'll come away cleanly. If you don't remove them, you'll discover it's a jungle in there!

If you are growing bush tomatoes, such as Garden Pearl – these types usually produce cherry tomatoes – you will not need to stake them or pinch out any side shoots.

Squash and sweetcorn

Courgettes Early in the month sow courgette seeds in the same way as cucumbers. Given how large the plants grow – at least 1m (3ft 3in) across, and how heavily they crop, decide how many you have room for. Four plants are plenty for a small garden.

Pumpkins These need a great deal of space, but are great fun to grow if only for Halloween.

Pumpkins are from the same family as courgettes so sow them in the same way inside now, ready to go outside at the end of the month in soil enriched with manure.

Sweetcorn This vegetable resents having its roots disturbed, so sow it in root trainers or biodegradable pots that can be planted out in their entirety at the end of the month. We sowed sweetcorn in the greenhouse. But in warm, sheltered gardens it can be sown outside, especially if you can protect it until the middle/end of the month.

Sweetcorn is wind-pollinated, which means that it is the wind, rather than insects that carries the pollen over from one plant to another. The pollination is carried out much more successfully if the sweetcorn is planted in a block rather than in rows. So allow 30-35cm (12-14in) between seeds or plants each way.

If you want to grow mini corn, choose a special variety such as Minipop and grow them 15cm (6in) apart. You can also harvest immature cobs of ordinary varieties sown closer together.

Support for tomatoes
Above, from far left
Young tomato plants ready to go into their final pots

Push in a bamboo cane alongside to support growth

When the tomato plant is 23cm (9in) high, attach it to the cane, using soft twine

You'll soon have healthy, leafy plants, ready to fruit later on in the summer

May

Asparagus Feuilletés

Serves 8

When a maître d' in a smart restaurant, full of flourish and foreign inflections, is pushing the fresh 'asparagoose', there is only one question to be asked. Is it English? Because English asparagus is without any doubt the best in the world.

I once asked my friend Sudhir Dhanani, who isn't English himself, but imports exotic fruits and vegetables from all round the world, did he agree? Quite positively, yes! American is good, Peruvian even better, but English wins by a mile.

Once called 'sparrow grass', but now affectionately known in the trade as simply 'grass', English asparagus has a painfully short season – just two months in May and June. So we all need to be on full asparagus alert and make absolutely sure we feast appropriately and not let the season whiz by.

Just steam it and pour melted butter over, or some vinaigrette, or just good olive oil with a squeeze of lemon. Perhaps my own favourite would be to accompany it with a fluffy foaming hollandaise, or else, as in this recipe, to encase it in very thin, crisp parcels of puff pastry filled with an Italian fonduta (creamy melted cheese). A lovely starter for a summer's lunch or supper party, followed by salmon for a main course with strawberries to finish.

For the filling

175g (6oz) fresh asparagus

175g (6oz) fontina or Gruyère cheese, in one piece

1 tablespoon freshly grated Parmesan, plus a little extra, to sprinkle

3 tablespoons crème fraîche

a few sprigs of watercress, to garnish

salt and freshly milled black pepper

For the pastry

1 x 375g pack fresh, ready-rolled puff pastry

flour, for dusting when rolling

2 large egg yolks, beaten with a tablespoon of milk

You will also need a large baking tray, 30 x 40cm (12 x 16in), lightly oiled.

First, remove the pastry from the fridge and let it come to room temperature (about 10 minutes). Meanwhile, wash the asparagus in cold water, then take each stalk in both hands and bend and snap off the woody end. Then, arrange the stalks in an opened fan steamer. Place the steamer in a frying pan or saucepan, pour in about 2.5cm (1in) of boiling water from the kettle, then add some salt, put a lid on and steam for 2-3 minutes or until they feel tender when tested with a skewer. After that, remove them from the steamer and allow them to cool. Then dry the stalks with kitchen paper and cut each one into 3, on the diagonal. Next, using a small sharp knife, remove the rind from the fontina or Gruyère and cut it into 1cm (½in) cubes. Then, in a small bowl mix the Parmesan, crème fraîche and add some salt and freshly milled black pepper.

Now carefully unroll the sheet of pastry on to a lightly floured work surface and cut it in half. Roll out one half until it measures 30 x 30cm (12 x 12in) and then cut that into four 15 x 15cm (6 x 6in) squares. Then repeat the rolling and cutting with the other piece of pastry so you end up with 8 squares in all. Next, you need to carefully brush the edges of 4 of the pastry squares with some of the beaten egg yolk and milk. Then divide half of the crème fraîche filling between the 4 pieces of pastry, about a dessertspoon into the centre of each square.

Next, lay about half the quantity of asparagus on top of the crème fraîche and several cubes of cheese tucked in between. Now pull up the opposite corners of each square to meet in the centre like an envelope. Carefully pinch the seams together to seal them and make a small hole in the centre of each one to allow the steam to escape. Then, using a fish slice, transfer the parcels to the baking tray and now make the other 4. Cover the parcels on the baking sheet with clingfilm and chill until you are ready to cook them. To do that, pre-heat the oven to gas mark 6, 200°C (400°F). Then brush each one with the remaining beaten egg mix and lightly sprinkle each one with some Parmesan. Bake on a high shelf for 20-25 minutes or until they are golden brown, serve garnished with a few sprigs of watercress.

Green Herb Soup

Serves 3-4

This soup adapts to any combination of fresh herbs – chives, mint, sage, tarragon, thyme, rosemary, sorrel or any others that are available in the kitchen garden.

25g (1oz) butter
6 thick spring onions (and their green tops), thinly sliced
175g (6oz) potatoes, scraped and cubed
150g (5oz) outside lettuce leaves, or spinach leaves, de-stalked and shredded
425ml (15fl oz) light vegetable or chicken stock
2 rounded tablespoons chopped fresh herbs
150ml (5fl oz) single cream
a generous squeeze of lemon juice
salt and freshly milled black pepper

Melt the butter in a medium pan, and stir in the thinly sliced spring onions and the cubed potatoes. Stir and cook over a gentle heat so the vegetables soften gently without browning. Now stir in the shredded lettuce (or spinach). Get it all nicely coated with butter. Then add the stock, bring to simmering point, cover and cook gently for about 10 minutes or just long enough for the potatoes to soften. Next, pour the contents of the saucepan into a blender. Add the chopped fresh herbs and the cream and blend until smooth. Return the purée to the pan and re-heat, tasting and flavouring with the lemon juice, salt and pepper. Serve piping hot.

Vinaigrette Dressing

Serves 4-6

For first harvested salad leaves, this is my favourite dressing.

1 rounded teaspoon sea salt
1 clove garlic, peeled
1 rounded teaspoon mustard powder
1 dessertspoon each balsamic vinegar and sherry vinegar
5 tablespoons extra virgin olive oil
freshly milled black pepper

Begin by placing the salt in a mortar and crush it quite coarsely, then add the garlic and, as you begin to crush it and it comes into contact with the salt, it will quickly break down into a purée. Next add the mustard powder and really work it in, giving it about 20 seconds of circular movements to get it thoroughly blended. After that, add some freshly milled black pepper. Now add the vinegars and work these in the same way, then add the oil, switch to a small whisk and give everything a really good, thorough whisking. Whisk again before dressing the salad.

Summer

June

Nothing says summer quite like strawberries, freshly shelled peas, the first new potatoes…

TASKS FOR JUNE

Harvest beetroot, borlotti beans, broad
beans, cabbages, carrots, dwarf French beans,
herbs, lettuces, onions, peas, potatoes,
radishes, redcurrants, rocket, runner beans,
spinach, spring onions, strawberries, turnips
Plant cabbages, cauliflowers, courgettes
Pot up strawberry runners
Protect brassicas
Sow beetroot, carrots, dwarf French beans,
herbs, lettuces, radishes, rocket, spinach,
spring onions, turnips

With June come salads in abundance, spinach, peas, young carrots, early beans and new potatoes. By the end of the month, the first courgettes may be ready to harvest, too. Things are moving on in the greenhouse as well. The early tomatoes will be ripening, while the first fruits on the peppers, aubergines and chillies will be starting to set (the tiny fruits developing from the flowers). It's easy to forget about planning ahead, but you must keep on sowing now to ensure the abundance of your crops does not peter out at the height of summer.

In the garden

Beans and peas

Borlotti beans Once the pods of the borlotti beans start to turn red, you can begin to harvest them but, if you want to dry some of them for use in the winter, set aside a couple of plants and make sure you don't pick any pods from them. If you do, the plant will start trying to reproduce itself again and that will delay the ripening of the existing beans. Keep them well watered in dry weather.

Broad beans You can start to harvest these now – pick the pods when they're still young, about a finger in thickness gives the best flavour.

Dwarf French beans Towards the end of the month, you can start to harvest the first of the dwarf French beans. Even if there is only a handful ready, it's better to pick and keep them in the fridge until you have enough than to leave them on the plant to continue growing and become tougher. Sow some more now to keep the supply going. Push two beans into the soil at each station and, if they both germinate, remove the weaker of the two.

Peas Harvest these regularly and do take a look under the foliage, too, as it's easy to miss a few pods, which will then mature and slow down the production of new ones. Once the plant has reproduced itself by setting seed, the plants will stop producing peas.

Seasonal splendour

Top left Carry on picking spinach – harvest individual leaves or cut the whole plant

Top right Time to dig up the first of the new potatoes

Below left As soon as the borlotti beans start to turn red you can eat them

Below right Even if there are just a few Dwarf French beans ready, pick them now and store in the fridge until there's enough for a meal

Summer magic

Far right Opening a pod to reveal a cluster of shiny green peas has to be one of summer's most special pleasures

Right Runner beans twine around the framework – their vivid red blooms bring cheer

Runner beans By the very end of the month, you might be able to start picking the first beans. The trick is to do so when they are still relatively flat, before the beans inside have started to swell and make the pods look knobbly. Once that happens, the pods become tougher. Keep the plants well watered, otherwise the flowers may not develop into pods. In dry weather they need about 8-9 litres to 1sq m (about 2 gallons to 10.8sq ft) every few days.

Brassicas and leafy greens

Brussels sprouts, cabbages, calabrese, cauliflowers, sprouting broccoli Where you have space, plant out late autumn/winter cabbages and cauliflowers sown in May for successive cropping, and a winter variety of red cabbage. Keep all young brassicas in the enviromesh cage well watered until established, and then water only if the weather is very dry. You should be able to start harvesting spring-sown white and red cabbages now.

Spinach Carry on harvesting as before, either picking individual leaves from each plant or cutting a whole plant. Continue to sow part-rows of a variety, such as Hector, which is resistant to bolting. Keeping the plants well watered in warm, dry weather also helps to prevent spinach from bolting.

Bulbs, roots and stems

Asparagus Once the ridges are about 20cm (8in) high, you can stop ridging up. The spears will be turning to fern now – they will be very spindly in their first season. Keep the bed well watered and free of weeds. Although careful preparation of the soil earlier in the year will mean that there should be no perennial weeds, annual weeds (their seeds are blown in on the wind), may well have germinated by now.

Beetroot Harvest the first of these while still small. Twisting off the leaves 2.5cm (1in) above the beet prevents them from 'bleeding' – losing red juice. Sow another part-row.

DELIA IN THE KITCHEN Peas

Fresh, shelled peas are one of the most delightful vegetables of all – young and tender, they melt in the mouth when cooked and taste wonderful raw. Sure, it takes a bit of time to shell them but, sitting by an open window or in the garden on a bright summer's day, shelling peas can be wonderful therapy. To cook young, fresh, shelled peas, first you will need 225g (8oz) in the pod per person. After shelling, pop them in a steamer with some salt and give them 1 minute before you bite one; they shouldn't take any longer than 2 minutes in all. If they are a bit older, they may need 3-4 minutes ■

Carrots Carry on harvesting, loosening the soil around them with a fork if you need to. When the most recent sowing is about 2.5cm (1in) high, sow another part-row.

Celery You will still need to water twice a week in dry spells to prevent it from becoming stringy.

Leeks Keep free of weeds and water only in very dry weather.

Onions Some of the onions may be large enough to harvest now. If the shoulders of the bulbs are not visible, carefully scrape away the soil to see if they are the size you want. Within reason, there is no 'correct' size. If a small onion is all you need, harvest one. Take care not to disturb the onions on either side more than necessary, as you will want them to grow on for harvesting later.

Parsnips In very dry weather, keep them watered. If the foliage is not looking particularly vigorous you can liquid-feed with a fertiliser such as seaweed extract but otherwise, leave them alone.

Potatoes The earlies should be in flower at the beginning of the month. If so, and the weather is dry, give them plenty of water – 15-20 litres per sq m (3-4 gallons per 10.8sq ft) – every 10 days or so. Depending on exactly when you planted them – earlies take about 14 weeks from planting to harvest – they might be ready at the end of the month. Check by scraping aside some of the soil. If most of the potatoes are smaller than a quail's egg, replace the soil and leave them for another week or so. When the maincrop varieties start to flower, check the size of those tubers. If they are about the size of a standard marble, start to water them at the ratio given above.

Radishes Keep harvesting on a daily basis, and also continue to sow a part-row every week to ensure a continuous supply.

Spring onions Keep pulling spring onions and, as you do with radishes, sow another part-row weekly to prolong the supply.

Turnips These are delicious harvested small – golf-ball size – and early sowings should be ready now. In light soil you should be able to pull them out, but in heavier soil you'll need to loosen the soil around them with a fork first. As turnips are members of the brassica family, you can eat the tops like spring greens. If the weather is cool and wet, sow another part-row. If it's hot and dry, though, the seed is unlikely to germinate without shelter (see page 85).

Watch out...
When potato flowers show, it's time to water

Salad leaves

Lettuces Keep harvesting and sowing some more outside.

Rocket Keep on picking and sowing part-rows, as before.

Squash and sweetcorn

Courgettes Like potatoes, these are greedy feeders, so they need a mix of well-rotted manure and compost. Plant them out at the beginning of the month, allowing about 1sq m (10.8sq ft) per plant. They may look small now, but don't be fooled – they will soon grow very large.

Initially, you may find that you get far more male flowers than female ones (the former are needed to pollinate the latter and make sure the fruits swell), which means the chances of successful pollination by insects are reduced.

You can easily tell the flowers apart because the male flowers have just a thin stem, while the female ones have an embryonic fruit at the base of the flower. Eventually, the plant will start to produce more female flowers, but you can help things along by picking a fully open male flower and pressing its stamens against the female's stigma to transfer pollen across.

To produce their fleshy fruits and large leaves, courgettes require plenty of water, so make sure that the soil never dries out. As soon as the first courgettes are about 10cm (4in) long, or the size of a cricket ball or large orange, if you are growing the Eight Ball variety, start picking and check the plants almost

DELIA IN THE KITCHEN Courgettes

Courgettes are baby marrows, and don't I know it!

If you are not vigilant about picking them every day in season, they seem to turn into marrows overnight – and marrow for supper night after night is not a good idea! Courgettes are a delicate vegetable, with not a great deal of their own flavour and, like aubergines, they have a high water content that can render them watery and dull. I like them chunkily cut and roasted in the oven or marinated in a vinaigrette with herbs (see page 80), which allows them to absorb some real flavour ■

Compare and contrast
Far left Gold Rush courgette in flower

Left The cricket-ball-size Eight Ball. Both varieties of courgette need manure-enriched soil and plenty of water

Ultra-fresh

Top left The sweetcorn is growing and a 'tassel' at the top of the stem is developing

Top right A fresh crop of carrots pulled straight from the soil

Below left Baby turnips – if you pick them small, the flavour is delicious

Below right For healthy salads any time grow All-The-Year-Round lettuces

every day. What is a small, immature courgette today will grow to be a mini-marrow in a few days' time.

Pumpkins To make the best use of space, train the trailing stems of the pumpkins along the edge of the bed, pegging them down with hoops of bent wire, if necessary. Water until the plants are well established, but after that they will be putting down roots as they trail, and can find the water they need unaided.

Sweetcorn In exposed gardens, earth up the plants a little (draw up the soil around them) to give them support and encourage the production of more roots to anchor them. Keep them free of weeds, either by mulching or by hand-weeding. Don't use a hoe since sweetcorn is shallow-rooted and you could damage the roots.

Soft-fruit bushes

Blackcurrants In their first season, don't expect a large crop. As the fruits turn colour, check that they don't go short of water.

Gooseberries Keep free of weeds and well watered. Watch out for gooseberry sawfly larvae – pale green caterpillar-like creatures with black markings – which, in Delia's kitchen garden, managed to defoliate the gooseberry bushes, more or less completely. The eggs were almost certainly present on the undersides of the leaves when the bushes were planted and, as the larvae hatched, they started feeding in the centre of the plant (where it was easy to miss them) and then worked their way out very rapidly. You often don't spot gooseberry sawfly until the damage has been done. The bushes will produce new leaves but the sawflies will produce new larvae and repeated defoliation affects the vigour of the bushes. You can spray against gooseberry sawfly with derris (a natural insecticide acceptable to organic gardeners). Or, if you don't like spraying at all, inspect the undersides of the leaves daily and remove any eggs or larvae you see.

Raspberries Keep them well watered and weed free.

Redcurrants These will also produce only a light crop in their first season. As the fruit is thin-skinned and easily squashed, cut off the strigs of fruit with scissors.

Soft fruit in pots

Blueberries Keep the compost moist – rain water is ideal. If you are watering with tap water in a limestone area, you may find the leaves take on a yellowish tinge. This is chlorosis, which is caused by too much alkalinity. Either add sulphur to the compost

Strawberry season
Far left In June early strawberries are starting to ripen

Left Potting up strawberry runners to produce new plants

according to the rate given on the packet, or water with a fertiliser specifically for acid-loving plants, such as Miracid.

Strawberries Earlier fruiting varieties, such as Gariguette and Elvira, should be cropping well and ready to pick from the middle of the month. Make sure the compost doesn't dry out, but water the compost, rather than the plants as, if the leaves are wet, particularly in the evening, there is more chance of fungal diseases.

If the plants are starting to produce runners – long stems with clusters of leaves at the end – cut them off, or, if you want to increase your stock of strawberry plants, to plant in the fruit cage for next year, pot them up. For each new plant, take a 9cm (3½in) pot of moist, soil-based compost and place it under the end cluster of leaves. To keep the leaves in close contact with the compost, secure the runner on the top of the compost with a hoop of wire, like a hairpin. Keep the compost moist, and the runner will form roots – and a new plant – in a few weeks. Once you can see new leaves appearing from the centre of the crown, you'll know it has rooted and you can sever the umbilical cord to separate it from the mother plant!

DELIA IN THE KITCHEN Strawberries

To get the most pleasure out of strawberries it's best to know how to treat them before you eat them. This means a bit of TLC, because their sheer beauty can be lost by bad handling.

1 Eat them the same day you pick them or store in a cool place with the hulls intact.

2 Fridges and strawberries don't like each other. Low temperatures rob them of fragrance and flavour and somehow transfer the flavour to other ingredients in the fridge (uncovered milk or cream can quickly absorb strawberry flavours).

3 Please don't wash them. They tend to absorb water, which makes them mushy, so this also means it's not a good idea to pick after heavy rain. Just wipe them with damp kitchen paper.

4 Leave the hulls in as long as possible and only remove them an hour or so before eating.

5 If you're forced to put them in the fridge, try sugared strawberries, which involves slicing them in half, sprinkling with caster sugar and storing them in a tightly lidded polythene box. During the storage the juices will mingle with the sugar and form a lovely strawberry-flavoured syrup. Remove from the fridge about an hour before serving ■

Setting the scene

Above left A vibrant display of Shirley poppies

Above right On the fig tree a few small green fruits are forming

Fruit trees

Apricots and peaches Do any final thinning of small, green fruits on peach trees and on apricot trees, if needed. This will help to encourage a plentiful crop of good-size fruit.

Figs By the end of this month, there will be new shoots along the length of the branches of the fig tree. Unless you need these shoots to grow and fill out the framework of the fan, pinch them back to five leaves.

On young trees, this will encourage embryo figs to form in each of the leaf joints to overwinter and ripen the following year. With more mature trees in warm gardens, you may have green figs already forming now, which will ripen and be harvested in the summer months during the same year.

Herbs

Basil, chervil, chives, coriander, mint, parsley, rosemary, sage, tarragon, thyme   Keep picking and sowing herbs through the summer to keep the supplies going. With almost all herbs, flowering affects the flavour and texture of the leaves, so try to remove the flowers as they appear or as soon as they start to fade to get the best flavour from your crop.

If you want to enjoy more chives, as soon as flowering is over, cut them back to about 5cm (2in) to encourage a new crop of leaves. Sage and thyme also benefit from a trim once flowering has finished.

The flowers of the tarragon plant are nothing special, so to boost leaf production, remove the spikes as soon as they appear.

Flowers

Convolvulus tricolor, cornflowers, love-in-a-mist (Nigella), California and Shirley poppies, pot marigold (Calendula) and the bishop's flower (Ammi majus) The more you keep picking, the more the flowers will grow. One tip with Shirley poppies, which are not usually considered a cut flower, is that if you sear the ends of the stalks with a lighter or over a gas ring as soon as you pick them, they will last a good few days in a vase. Pick the sweet peas growing with the runner beans too.

In the greenhouse

Fruiting vegetables

Aubergines When the plants are about 20cm (8in) tall, pinch out the growing tips – the top centimetre or so – on the main shoot. This encourages them to produce side shoots, making bushier plants that are easier to support.

Chillies and sweet peppers Once the fruits appear – they will be green at this stage – feed weekly with tomato fertiliser to encourage more flowers and therefore fruits.

Cucumbers The first of these should be starting to ripen. Don't be tempted to pick them too soon or they may well taste bitter. It is essential that the compost never dries out. If the leaves look pale, feed with a liquid fertiliser until they look greener again.

Tomatoes Tie them to the canes every 15-20cm (6-8in) or so and be vigilant about pinching out the side shoots that appear in the leaf axils. Once the first truss (cluster of minute green tomatoes) appears, start feeding with tomato fertiliser once a week. With watering, strike a happy medium – too much and the flavour is diluted, too little water and the crop suffers. There won't be many insects to pollinate the flowers inside, so tap the canes sharply with a stick to shake the pollen loose and on to the neighbouring flowers.

Salad leaves

Lettuces Growing a few plants in the greenhouse is a good insurance policy – you'll have instant fillers to hand if you find that there's going to be a bit of a gap in the outdoor sowings.

Flowers first
The mauve flower of the aubergine plant

Mid-summer display In June you can cut and appreciate the sight and scent of the sweet peas that are growing with the runner beans

June

Home-made Strawberry Preserve

Makes 3 x 350ml (1lb) jars

Strawberries are plentiful in the summer, so why not take advantage of this by storing away some of their sunny, ripe flavour to brighten bleak winter days to come? In a preserve, the whole fruit is suspended intact in its own jelly, so none of the lusciousness is lost. The way to keep strawberries whole in jam is to cover them with the sugar and leave them overnight. The sugar will then draw out the juices and firm the fruit.

900g (2lb) slightly under-ripe strawberries
700g (1lb 8oz) preserving sugar
juice of 1 large lemon
10g (½oz) butter

You will also need a preserving pan, 3 x 350ml (1lb) jars, plus waxed discs to seal.

First of all, hull the strawberries and wipe each one with kitchen paper. Then layer them into a preserving pan, sprinkling them with sugar as you go. Leave them to soak in the sugar overnight, giving everything a stir around before you go to bed.

When you're ready to make the preserve, put 4 small plates into the freezer. Place the pan over a fairly low heat and allow the sugar to dissolve slowly. Give the pan a shake from time to time, but only give very gentle stirs, as you want to try very hard not to break up the fruit. To check if the sugar is dissolved, lift up the spoon and, if there are no little crystals of sugar visible on it, the mixture is ready for boiling.

Now turn the heat up to its highest setting, add the lemon juice and as soon as the mixture is up to what old-fashioned cooks used to call a rolling boil, put the timer on for 8 minutes exactly. Then, when the 8 minutes are up, remove the mixture from the heat, put a teaspoonful on to one of the chilled plates, allow it to cool, then push the mixture with your little finger. If a crinkly skin has formed on the jam and there is no liquid left, then the preserve is set. Allow the preserve to settle for 15 minutes, adding the butter if there's any scum, then pour into jars that have been washed, dried and heated in a moderate oven for 5 minutes to sterilise. Seal immediately with waxed discs, then cover with the lids or Cellophane and elastic bands. Wait until the preserve is completely cold, then label the jars.

Note: try not to wash strawberries or attempt to make jam after it has rained heavily and the fruit is wet – it must be as dry as possible. If you are forced to wash the fruit, dry it and spread it out on clean tea cloths to dry further before using. Any extra moisture will dilute the pectin and make setting more difficult.

Marinated Courgette and Coriander Salad

Serves 2

Courgettes grow like the clappers – fast. So you have to be vigilant and collect them every day or you just end up with huge marrows, and while the odd marrow is not to be despised, too many marrows can be a problem, especially as most country people are desperate to give them away at this time of year.

Courgettes harvested young and tender are perfect in this salad, based on the classic *à la grècque* theme – serve it as a starter with chunks of sourdough bread or as an accompaniment to grilled chicken or fish.

350g (12oz) small courgettes

1 heaped teaspoon coriander seeds

3 tablespoons olive oil

1 medium red onion, chopped small

1 clove garlic, crushed

6 black peppercorns

1 tablespoon white wine vinegar

6 tablespoons white wine

juice of 1 small lemon

1 large, very red, ripe tomato,

skinned (see page 114) and chopped

1 tablespoon chopped fresh coriander leaves

and a few extra sprigs for serving

salt

You will also need a frying pan with a lid.

First, place the frying pan over a medium heat and, as soon as it gets hot, measure the coriander seeds straight into it. What they need now is to dry-roast, and this will take 1-2 minutes.

Shake the pan from time to time to toss them around a bit and, as soon as they start to jump, remove them from the heat and tip them straight into a mortar.

Now place the pan back over the heat and, as soon as it is hot, add 2 tablespoons of the olive oil and gently soften the onion and garlic in it for about 10 minutes.

Next, coarsely crush the coriander seeds, along with the peppercorns, using a pestle. Now measure the wine vinegar and wine and pour this in to join the onion, along with the crushed coriander and peppercorns, the lemon juice and a little salt. Bring it all up to a simmer and then turn the heat down and simmer gently for 5 minutes.

To prepare the courgettes: don't peel them, just wipe each one, trim off the ends and cut into 2.5cm (1in) diagonal or round chunks.

Now add these to the sauce, together with the chopped tomato, then stir well, put the lid on and simmer over a gentle heat for about 15 minutes, or until they're tender but still retain some 'bite'.

Next, carefully stir in the fresh coriander leaves, transfer the whole lot to a serving dish to cool, then cover and chill until you need it but don't forget to bring it back to room temperature for about 30 minutes before serving.

Drizzle with the remaining tablespoon of oil and garnish with the sprigs of coriander.

Young Carrots with Tarragon Butter

Serves 4

Instead of tarragon butter, a mixture of 3 finely chopped spring onions and 1 tablespoon of cream can be tossed in at the end of the cooking time.

450g (1lb) young small carrots,

washed, but left whole

25g (1oz) softened butter

1 teaspoon chopped fresh tarragon leaves

salt and freshly milled black pepper

Place the carrots in a steamer fitted over a saucepan of simmering water. Sprinkle them with salt, then steam them until tender – about 10-15 minutes, depending on their thickness and how crunchy you like them.

Meanwhile, mix the butter with the tarragon and some freshly milled black pepper, then when the carrots are ready, toss them in the tarragon mixture so that each one gets a light glistening of butter.

July

There are plenty of delicious crops to enjoy and a host of bright and cheery flowers to pick

TASKS FOR JULY

Harvest apricots, beetroot, blackcurrants, blueberries, borlotti beans, broad beans, cabbages, calabrese, carrots, cauliflowers, courgettes, cucumbers, dwarf French beans, figs, gooseberries, lettuces, onions, peaches, peas, potatoes, radishes, raspberries, redcurrants, rocket, runner beans, spinach, spring onions, strawberries, sweetcorn, sweet peppers, turnips

Pick flowers

Plant cauliflowers

Protect celery

Sow beetroot, cabbages, carrots, radishes, spring onions, turnips

July is another abundant month – you will find yourself spoilt for choice. There will still be plenty of spinach, the last of the peas, young carrots, lots of borlotti and runner beans and new potatoes. The rest of the International Kidney potatoes can be dug and the first of the Belle de Fontenay might be ready as well.

The courgettes will be in full swing, as will the greenhouse crops – tomatoes, cucumbers and sweet peppers. The aubergines will be starting to swell but probably won't have fully taken on that characteristic rich purple colour quite yet. If you have planted annuals, they should be in full bloom.

In the garden

Beans and peas

Borlotti beans These will still be cropping nicely. Harvest every day and water in dry weather. Remember, if you are saving some borlotti beans for drying, don't pick any pods from those plants.

Broad beans Continue to harvest.

Dwarf French beans Harvest on a daily basis this month. Keep the beans well watered in dry weather, and don't let the soil dry out.

Peas As the peas finish cropping, cut the plants at soil level and remove the top growth, along with the pea sticks. The roots of legumes have nodules that contain nitrogen. These are of great benefit to leafy brassicas, which you will plant in the same area of the kitchen garden afterwards. Save the pea sticks and put the peas' top growth into the compost bin.

Runner beans They should be plentiful now, and you may be at the point of supplying the neighbours as well as yourself. Do keep picking, though, because if too many pods are left to mature, the plant will stop producing new flowers and your runner-bean season will come to a premature end.

Give the beans plenty of water at this time of year. In dry weather they need about 8-9 litres to 1sq m (about 2 gallons to just over 10.8sq ft) every few days.

Bring on the beans
Far left Runner beans are plentiful and must be picked regularly, or the plants will stop producing

Left The red and white flowers of Painted Lady Improved beans are very attractive

Brassicas and leafy greens

Cabbages Harvest summer white and red cabbages and plant out any remaining seedlings for late autumn and winter.

Calabrese Cut the central head to eat while the buds are still tight and green and haven't begun to turn yellow as they start to flower. Leave the plants in the ground, and in a few weeks you will be rewarded with smaller side shoots that taste just as delicious.

Cauliflowers Harvest while the curds are still tightly packed and white and plant out any remaining seedlings.

Spinach Carry on harvesting. Keep the plants well watered in warm, dry weather, to help prevent it from bolting. Do not sow any spinach this month. The weather will probably be too hot and dry for it to germinate.

Bulbs, roots and stems

Asparagus Keep the bed free of weeds and make sure the soil doesn't dry out. If yours is a very windy garden, you may need to stake the asparagus fern to prevent damage to the crowns.

Beetroot Carry on harvesting and sow another part-row.

Carrots Carry on harvesting them. There's still time to sow another part-row. You could try a later variety, such as Autumn King, or the carrot-fly-resistant Flyaway F1.

Celery Keep the plants watered constantly and free of weeds. If you are growing a trench variety (as opposed to a self-blanching variety), you need to start blanching the plants when they are about 20-25.5cm (8-10in) tall. In the old days, people grew celery in trenches and used soil to exclude the light and keep the stems pale – that's why you used to buy celery with mud still attached. Some gardeners still do it this way but it is easier to grow the plants in a flat bed, then wrap a couple of sheets of newspaper around each plant and slip a 30cm (12in) length of plastic drainpipe over the newspaper (see page 96).

Leeks Keep the weeds at bay and only water if very dry.

Onions Carry on harvesting throughout the month, to use straightaway rather than store.

Parsnips Check the soil doesn't dry out in hot weather. If the roots are left to get very dry and are then watered, they may split.

Potatoes Harvest the rest of the new potatoes (International Kidney variety), and, perhaps at the very end of the month, the

Perfectly formed Summer cauliflowers are ready when the curds are tightly packed and white

Welcome sight

Far left Once the pumpkin plant has small fruits, take out the growing tip

Centre There are plenty of onions ready to eat immediately

Left Pull away the husk of sweetcorn and test for ripeness – push your nail into a kernel, and if milky juice spurts out, the corn is ripe

first of the Belle de Fontenay variety will be ready, too.

As you dig the potatoes out, you can put the top growth on the compost heap. When you clear a crop, make sure that you dig all the potatoes out of the soil to avoid all risk of blight developing in 'volunteers' – plants that will grow next year from any tubers left behind. You should start again next year with fresh seed potatoes certified to be free of disease. Keep the remaining potatoes well watered, making sure you water the soil not the foliage.

Radishes Keep harvesting and also, continue sowing a part-row every week to ensure a continuous supply.

Spring onions As you do with radishes, pull them as you need them and sow more.

Turnips Keep harvesting them now, while they are still reasonably small. These do not germinate if the temperature is above 25°C (77°F), so, if you want to make sowings now, try resting a plank on two small blocks of wood above the drill to create shade and keep the temperature down.

Salad leaves

Lettuces Harvest as they are ready. Like turnips, they do not germinate well in hot, dry weather. So, if these are the conditions, wait, or sow lettuces in moist soil under a raised plank (see above). Also plant out any seedlings sown in the greenhouse in June.

Rocket Pick the leaves as you need them. If the plants are looking rather tired, remove them. Rocket does not germinate well in very hot weather, so don't sow any more for a month or so.

Squash and sweetcorn

Courgettes Continue to pick the courgettes every day or two and keep them well watered.

Pumpkins Once each plant has small fruits setting at the base of three flowers (or two if you're aiming for giant pumpkins), take out the growing tip (the tip at the end of the longest shoot). This means the plant can put its strength into swelling the fruits.

Sweetcorn In dry weather, once the male flowers or 'tassels' on the tops of the stems appear and the pods begin to swell, water the plants well. Tackle any weeds that appear, remembering to hand-weed and not use a hoe, which could damage the shallow roots. In an exceptionally good summer, and in a very sheltered garden, the cobs may be ready to pick at the end of the month. If they feel like a good size, carefully peel back the husk to expose the corn inside and see if it is golden in colour and ripe. Press your nail into a kernel – if the sweetcorn is ripe, a milky juice will spurt out. To pick the cob, support the stem with one hand and, with the other, snap the cob off with a sharp downward movement. If the cob is not ripe, carefully replace the husk and wait for a week or so.

DELIA IN THE KITCHEN
Sweetcorn

By far the best and most delicious way to cook and eat corn on the cob is to strip off the green casing and all the silky threads, toss the cobs in a little olive oil, season well with salt and black pepper and roast on an open barbecue. Watch them carefully, turning them all the time, until they're toasted golden brown – 5-10 minutes. You will need one medium head of corn per person ∎

Soft-fruit bushes

Remove any weeds that appear in the fruit cage. Prune some of the container-grown bushes planted in the spring. The point of pruning is to remove old, unproductive wood, to encourage production of new wood and heavy crops next summer and beyond.

Blackcurrants Pick as they come ripe – unlike older varieties, the Ben Connan tends to ripen all the berries on a strig at the same time – keep the bushes well watered, making sure you don't splash the foliage. There is no need to prune container-grown blackcurrants in the first season but they will need pruning in future years.

Gooseberries and redcurrants Pick ripe fruit and keep watered. If newly established redcurrants are growing well, start summer pruning. Leave the main shoot from which the side shoots grow – then shorten all the other shoots coming off it to five leaves. With gooseberries, shorten the side shoots by half. This encourages the plants to produce fruiting spurs rather than non-productive shoots and leaves. It also removes much of the soft, sappy growth that attracts pests such as aphids. From the second year onwards, both gooseberries and redcurrants will need pruning in the spring and in the summer.

Raspberries Harvest any berries as they ripen and turn red.

Soft fruit in pots

Blueberries Keep them watered, as before. The fruits should be taking on their smokey blue colour but, obviously, in the first year, you won't get very many.

Strawberries While earlier fruiting varieties, such as Gariguette and Elvira, should be over by this time, the mid-to-late-summer ones, such as Florence, should be producing well. Continue to water, as before. If you have potted up all the runners you need, remove any new ones, as leaving them will weaken the parent plant. Make sure that the potted-up runners don't dry out.

DELIA IN THE KITCHEN
Raspberries

A truly exquisite soft fruit that needs hardly any adornment. I like them served on a plate spread out in a single layer with a minute sprinkling of sugar, and I eat them just like that as often as I can during the season. Treat them more or less like strawberries – no water if possible, and covered if you're forced to keep them in the fridge. Raspberries, like strawberries, also lend themselves to countless recipe ideas. Damaged, over-soft fruits make marvellous tarts, and, if you sieve them and add icing sugar to taste, you have a wonderful sauce for pouring over ice cream or strawberries ■

Fruit trees

Apricots Depending on the variety, these should start to ripen by the end of the month. You can tell when they're ready by the rich apricot colour and the fact that the fruits feel soft. Like peaches, they don't store well, so eat them rightaway.

Figs Once the fruits are dark brown, soft to touch, are hanging down and the skin is just starting to split, they are ready to pick. To do this, hold on to the stalk and snap it away from the shoot.

Peaches Peaches should start to ripen by the end of July, depending on the variety planted. To test, cup the fruit in your hand, and with your fingers gently press around the stalk. If it gives under pressure, the peach is ripe. Pick it carefully to avoid bruising.

Flowers

Convolvulus tricolor, cornflowers, love-in-a-mist (Nigella), California and Shirley poppies, pot marigold (Calendula) and the bishop's flower (Ammi majus) The annuals should still be flowering well, so pick regularly for more flowers.

In the greenhouse
Brassicas and leafy greens

Cabbages Sow spring cabbage now for overwintering and harvesting next spring.

Fruiting vegetables

Aubergines The secret here, as with all greenhouse crops, is to be consistent with watering and feed once a week with tomato fertiliser. The fruits will be swelling and turning purple.

Chillies The first fruits should be a decent size now and may just be turning colour. The redder they are, the hotter they are.

Cucumbers Start to harvest these now, taking the lowest, most mature fruits first.

Sweet peppers You should have some decent-size fruits, although still green. Harvest the lower ones, even if you prefer them red, to encourage the plant to go on flowering and produce more fruits.

Tomatoes Continue to tie the stems to the supporting cane every 15-20cm (6-8in). As soon as the plants have four trusses of fruit (or flowers in the case of the top ones), pinch out the growing tip two leaves above the highest truss. Keep pinching out side shoots that appear at the point where the leaves join the stem.

Spoilt for choice

Top left Luscious green gooseberries are part of the summer harvest

Top right Broad beans ready for shelling

Below left Pick peaches carefully to avoid bruising them

Below right The gleaming fruits of the aubergine are ripening

July

Braised Peas, Rocket and Spring Onions

Serves 6

This is a good recipe for slightly older peas, which, in my opinion, sometimes have more texture and flavour than the younger ones. However, if the peas you are using are very young, give them far less cooking time – 8 minutes at the most.

1.35kg (3lb) peas (unshelled weight), freshly shelled

60g (2½oz) fresh rocket

12 bulbous spring onions

40g (1½oz) butter

a pinch of golden caster sugar

1 rounded teaspoon sea salt

First, trim the spring onions: you need only the white bulbs (the rest can be chopped and saved for something such as a stir-fry). Pull off any thick, stalky bits from the rocket and tear the larger leaves in half. Now all you do is put all the ingredients in a large saucepan, together with 3 tablespoons of water, cover with a lid, bring them up to simmering point and simmer gently for 8-15 minutes, depending on the age of the peas.

Broad Bean Salad with Pancetta and Sherry Vinegar

Serves 4 generously

The broad bean season seems to be so short, I always feel the need to feast as much as possible when I can, hence this salad. It's good as a first course or served with other salads in a cold buffet. This recipe can also be made with shelled, fresh borlotti beans – cooking the beans for 20-25 minutes instead of 5.

1.8kg (4lb) young broad beans, shelled

110g (4oz) sliced smoked pancetta or smoked streaky bacon

1 tablespoon chopped mixed fresh herbs (parsley, chives, basil and thyme, for example)

2 shallots, finely chopped

salt and freshly milled black pepper

For the dressing

2 tablespoons sherry vinegar

1 large clove garlic

2 teaspoons sea salt

2 teaspoons mustard powder

5 tablespoons extra virgin olive oil

Begin this by pre-heating the grill to its highest setting for 10 minutes or so, then place the pancetta (or bacon) on a piece of foil and grill it 7.5cm (3in) from the heat for 3-4 minutes; it's important to get it really crisp. Then, as soon as it's cool enough to handle, crumble it into tiny pieces.

Now place the shelled beans in a medium saucepan, add a teaspoon of salt and pour in enough boiling water to barely cover them. When they come back to the boil, put a lid on, turn the heat down and simmer them gently for about 5 minutes. It's very important not to overcook them, so a timer would be useful here.

While they're cooking, make the dressing by first crushing the garlic and salt with a pestle and mortar until it becomes a creamy paste, then work in the mustard powder and follow this with the vinegar and a generous amount of coarsely milled black pepper. Next, add the oil and give everything a good whisk. When the beans are cooked, drain them in a colander, then place them in a serving bowl, toss them in the dressing and give it all a good stir. Now sprinkle in the pancetta (or bacon), herbs and chopped shallots, taste to check the seasoning, give everything one more good mix, then cover the bowl with a cloth and leave aside for a couple of hours so the beans can absorb all the flavours.

Buttered New Potatoes with Parsley, Mint and Chives

Serves 4

Made with home-grown new potatoes, these are so good you could eat a plateful all by themselves!

900g (2lb) new potatoes
1 tablespoon chopped fresh parsley
1 sprig of fresh mint
1 tablespoon snipped fresh chives
40g (1½oz) softened butter
2 tablespoons chopped fresh mint
sea salt and freshly milled black pepper

Wash but don't scrape the potatoes as there are a lot of nutrients as well as flavour in the skins. Place the larger ones over the base of the saucepan and pop the smaller ones on top. Pour in enough boiling water to not quite cover, add some salt and the sprig

of mint. Cover with a tight-fitting lid, and simmer gently for about 20 minutes. Test them with a skewer, and remember they must be tender but still firm – overcooking really does spoil them. Alternatively, steam them, sprinkling them with salt and tucking the mint in among them. Meanwhile, mix the butter and herbs thoroughly together with some pepper. Then drain the cooked potatoes, add the herb butter, put the lid back on and swirl the pan around to get each one thoroughly coated. Remove the lid and just savour the delicious aroma for a couple of seconds before you dish them out!

A Summer Trifle with Raspberries and Raspberry Purée

Serves 6

No cooking involved here – just a quick assembly job, but when you come to eat it you won't believe it could be that easy.

5 trifle sponges
350g (12oz) fresh raspberries
2 rounded tablespoons raspberry jam
120ml (4fl oz) Madeira
½ tablespoon golden caster sugar
250g (9oz) mascarpone
1 x 500ml tub fresh ready-made custard
1 tablespoon toasted flaked almonds

You will also need a 1.75-litre (3-pint) glass trifle bowl.

First of all, cut the trifle sponges in half lengthways, spread each half with raspberry jam, then re-form them and cut each one into 3 little sandwiches. Now arrange them in the bowl. Then make a few stabs in the sponges and sprinkle the Madeira carefully and evenly over them, then leave it all aside for half an hour to soak in.

After that sprinkle half the raspberries over the top of the sponges, pushing some down in among them. Then put the rest into a food processor, along with the sugar, and whiz to a purée, then push the purée through a nylon sieve to remove the pips. Next, drizzle the purée over the raspberries. Now empty the mascarpone into a bowl, give it a whisk to soften it, then add the custard, a little at a time, whisking them together till thoroughly blended. Spoon the mixture evenly over the top of the raspberries and sprinkle with toasted flaked almonds.

Blueberry and Pecan American Muffins

Makes 20 mini muffins

I love American home cooking, and one of the things I feel Americans are particularly good at is baking. The American muffin reigns supreme – not like the British bread version but more like superior fairy cakes and oh so much easier to make and more of a treat. Like many other things in America, they used to come big, but now that calorie counting is here to stay there are mini versions, which means you can make lots of different bite-sized flavours.

110g (4oz) small blueberries

50g (2oz) pecan nuts, finely chopped

150g (5oz) plain flour

½ tablespoon baking powder

¼ teaspoon salt

1 large egg

40g (1½oz) golden caster sugar

120ml (4fl oz) milk

50g (2oz) butter, melted and cooled slightly

½ teaspoon pure vanilla extract

For the topping

50g (2oz) pecan nuts, finely chopped

10 demerara sugar cubes, crushed

You will also need 2 mini-muffin trays. The muffins can be baked with or without cake papers, which simply help to keep them fresh.

Pre-heat the oven to gas mark 6, 200°C (400°F).

Start off by sifting the flour, baking powder and salt into a large bowl. Then, in a separate bowl, mix together the egg, sugar, milk, melted butter and vanilla extract. Now return the dry ingredients to the sieve and sift them straight on to the egg mixture (this double sifting is essential because there won't be much mixing going on). What you need to do now is take a large spoon and fold the dry ingredients into the wet ones – quickly, in about 15 seconds. Don't be tempted to beat or stir, and don't be alarmed by the rather unattractive, uneven appearance of the mixture: this, in fact, is what will ensure that the muffins stay light.

Now fold the blueberries and pecan nuts into the mixture, again with a minimum of stirring: just a quick folding in. Spoon in just enough mixture to fill each muffin cup (if you're not using papers, grease the tins well), then top with chopped pecans and crushed sugar. Bake on a high shelf of the oven for 20 minutes or until well risen and brown. Remove the muffins from the oven and cool in the tins for 5 minutes before transferring to a wire rack (if they are in paper cases remove them from the tins straightaway).

Gooseberry Yoghurt Fool

Serves 6

I now find that lusciously thick genuine Greek yoghurt makes the best fruit fool of all, as it allows the full flavour of the fruit to dominate. If you're serving this to someone who doesn't like yoghurt, don't worry – they won't know.

900g (2lb) gooseberries, topped and tailed with scissors

275g (10oz) Greek yoghurt

150g (5oz) golden caster sugar

You will also need a shallow, 23cm (9in) square or round, ovenproof baking dish and 6 serving glasses, each with a capacity of 175ml (6fl oz).

Pre-heat the oven to gas mark 4, 180°C (350°F).

For the fullest flavour, I think gooseberries are best cooked in the oven. So first place them in the baking dish, sprinkle on the sugar and bake them on the centre shelf of the oven, uncovered, for 20-30 minutes, or until tender when tested with a skewer.

After that, tip them into a sieve set over a bowl to drain off the excess juice. Now reserve about a quarter of the cooked gooseberries for later, then place the rest in the bowl of a food processor, add 4 tablespoons of the reserved juice and whiz to a thick purée. After that, leave the purée to get quite cold, then empty the yoghurt into a bowl, give it a stir, then fold in half the purée. Now spoon this mixture into the serving glasses, spoon the rest of the purée on top and, finally, add the reserved gooseberries. Cover the glasses with clingfilm and chill till you're ready to serve.

August

In the heat of late summer, make the most of crisp salad crops and ripe fruiting vegetables

TASKS FOR AUGUST

Harvest apricots, beetroot, blueberries, borlotti beans, broad beans, cabbages, calabrese, carrots, cauliflowers, chillies, courgettes, cucumbers, figs, dwarf French beans, leeks, lettuces, parsnips, peaches, potatoes, radishes, raspberries, rocket, runner beans, spinach, spring onions, strawberries, sweetcorn, sweet peppers, tomatoes, turnips

Pick flowers

Plant cabbages

Sow chard, lettuces, mizuna, mustard spinach, pak choi, radicchio, radishes, rocket, spinach, spinach beet, turnips

August, while still very abundant, marks the beginning of the end of summer. Some crops, such as peas, have already finished, while others, like onions, will be ready for lifting. Salad crops – lettuces, radishes and so on – continue to be harvested and sown, along with other vegetables, such as chard, and towards the end of the month, you can start off oriental greens – mustard spinach, pak choi and mizuna greens – for autumn and winter. Since many will bolt in hot, dry weather, late summer is a good time to sow them. They will withstand some frost and with the protection of a cloche will give you crops through the autumn and into the winter.

In the garden

Beans

Borlotti beans Keep them well watered and harvest all except those that you are keeping to dry.

Broad beans These beans will be finishing now, so harvest the last pods.

Dwarf French beans Carry on harvesting them and, as before, keep the soil moist.

Runner beans They should be cropping so well that even the true lover of the runner bean may well have reached saturation point! If you are going away on holiday, ask a friend or neighbour to come in during your absence to help themselves to beans (and to water them well in dry weather), so that when you come back, there will still be plenty. If the beans aren't picked, the existing pods will become tough and inedible and the plants will stop producing.

Brassicas and leafy greens

Cabbages Harvest as they are ready. Plant out some spring cabbages for next year. If you are planning to eat them as spring greens, as well as fully grown cabbages, plant them about 10cm (4in) apart in rows at a distance of 30cm (12in) apart. Then next spring you can harvest two out of every three plants to use as spring greens, leaving the third to heart up as a cabbage.

It's a fair crop This is peak time for fresh green beans and there are plenty of potatoes to cook or store

Progress report
Far right Make sure
your celery is slug free

Right Carry on
harvesting young
spinach leaves

Calabrese Harvest the smaller side shoots that the plants will have produced after the central head was cut. As soon as a plant has stopped producing, pull it out, chop it up and compost it.

Cauliflowers Continue to harvest.

Chard Bright Lights chard is strikingly pretty as well as delicious with rich, green leaves and tender stems in a range of colours – bright red, pink, violet and yellow. Treat it as a cut-and-come-again crop for salads or stir-fries, or cook it like spinach. Chard is usually sold as multigerm seed. The seeds are large enough to sow individually, about 5cm (2in) apart and in rows 45cm (18in) apart.

Spinach Carry on harvesting. Sow half a row of a hardy variety, such as San Marco or Samish F1, for an autumn crop if the weather is mild or for overwintering and harvesting in the spring.

Spinach beet This is a relative of beetroot but it is grown for its leaves. It's easier to grow than spinach – hardier and less likely to bolt. It is usually sold as multigerm seeds, like chard. Sow individually, in rows, as for chard. It is harvested in the autumn.

Bulbs, roots and stems

Asparagus Keep the bed weed free and watered, as before. Towards the end of the month the asparagus fern will be starting to turn yellow, but leave it until it has completely died and turned brown. The fern will then be ready to cut down next month.

Beetroot Continue harvesting as needed.

Carrots Carry on pulling the carrots. If the seedlings are through from the varieties sown last month, you can thin them now.

Celery If your plants weren't large enough to start blanching last month, do it now. Check from time to time that your plastic drainpipes are not harbouring slugs and snails.

Leeks You can start harvesting this month if you want to, but if you feel that the leeks are more an autumn and winter vegetable, they will also stay in the ground in excellent condition.

Onions Once the foliage turns yellow and flops over, the remaining onions are ready for lifting and storing for use over the next few months. Lift them carefully to avoid any damage to the bulbs and leave them to dry.

In very dry weather you can leave them on the soil to dry in the sun, turning them from time to time, or better still, lay them on a drying rack – a piece of chicken wire stapled to four short posts is ideal, enabling the air to circulate all round them. When they are bone dry – the papery skins should rustle – store them. You can either plait the dead leaves together à la French onion seller, or trim off the tops and place them in onion nets – those orange nylon nets the greengrocer buys his onions in are ideal (ask your greengrocer for a couple). Old, fine fishnet tights are another option! Hang the onions in a cool, dry but light place.

Parsnips The first roots may be ready this month, although parsnips often taste sweeter after the first frosts, which means leaving them until next month or even the month after.

Potatoes Harvest Pink Fir Apple and Belle de Fontenay as they are ready and check on the progress of Desirée by scraping away a little of the soil at the side of the ridge. Any tubers that are large enough can be harvested but you can leave most of the Desirée crop to bulk up for a few more weeks.

Depending on their size, Belle de Fontenay may benefit from being left for a week or so, too. If you are plagued with slugs, though, it might be better to harvest all the potatoes now and store them in paper sacks in a cool, dark place.

Radishes Keep harvesting and sowing more seeds regularly.

For salads A crop of Pink Fir Apple potatoes are ready for the pot

DELIA IN THE KITCHEN
Beetroot

Prepare a bunch of small summer beetroot by leaving the trailing root intact but trimming the green stalk so only 2.5cm (1in) is left. Wash well under cold, running water, but leave the peel on. Place it in a medium saucepan, then add salt and enough boiling water to barely cover. Simmer, covered, for 20-30 minutes, until the skin eases away when pushed away with your thumbs. Peel and serve hot as a vegetable or cold with vinaigrette in a salad ■

Raising the root
Far left Twisting off the beetroot leaves about 2.5cm (1in) above the beets will stop them from 'bleeding'

Left There are still plenty of juicy orange carrots left to pull up

Spring onions Carry on harvesting. Seed sown now will not crop until spring next year, so if you are going to re-sow make sure you choose a winter-hardy variety.

Turnips Carry on harvesting. These vegetables are, in fact, a member of the cabbage family and turnips tops are very tasty so, if you want to grow some for autumn/winter greens, you might want to sow a row now. If you harvest the leaves (turnip tops), you will be taking the roots' source of food, so don't expect a decent crop of turnips from the same plants. You have to choose one or the other.

Oriental greens

Mizuna Sow thinly in drills 1cm (½in) deep in rows 23cm (9in) apart. Unless you plan to use it all as baby leaves, towards the end of the month, thin the seedlings to 10cm (4in) apart and eat the thinnings. If the seedlings are not large enough to thin, leave them until next month.

Mustard spinach Sow and thin as you do mizuna.

Pak choi Station sow two or three seeds of pak choi 2cm (¾in) deep, 10cm (4in) apart and in rows 45cm (18in) apart.

Salad leaves

Lettuces Pick and keep sowing. Both All The Year Round and Lobjoits are reasonably hardy and seed sown early in the month will give you a mid-autumn crop. If it is very hot, use the plank technique (see page 85).

Radicchio This dramatic, deep red and cream salad vegetable with streaked, striped or speckled leaves has a tangy, pleasantly bitter flavour. It is relatively hardy, so by sowing some now, and protecting it in the autumn, you can eat it through the winter as a salad leaf or cooked. Sow half a row – thinly, if you plan to use it as a cut-and-come-again crop or, if you want the plants to heart up, station sow about 10cm (4in) apart and, once the seedlings are up, thin to 30cm (12in). Use the thinnings in salads.

DELIA IN THE KITCHEN New potatoes

The best way I have found to retain the flavour of potatoes is not to boil them at all but to steam them. Firstly, pour boiling water from the kettle into a pan fitted with a fan steamer, then place the potatoes in the steamer, sprinkle with salt (about 1 rounded teaspoon per 450g/1lb) and tuck in a few sprigs of mint. Then put a tight lid on and let them cook in the steam till tender – 12-15 minutes. The best way to test whether they are tender is to use a thin skewer inserted in the thickest part. After that, drain off any water beneath the steamer, then place a cloth over the potatoes for 5 minutes, which will absorb some of the excess steam that tends to cling to the potatoes and make them soggy ∎

Shaping up

Top left Ripe tomatoes cut fresh from the vine

Top right The aubergine has taken on its typical dark purple colour

Below left A sweet green pepper – you can eat it now or leave it to redden

Below right Chillies vary in strength and colour – the red ones are more fiery

Rocket Keep on picking and at the end of the month when the weather starts to cool down a little, start sowing part-rows again.

Squash and sweetcorn

Courgettes As long as they are producing, keep on harvesting. In very dry weather you may find powdery white patches appearing on the leaves. This is a mildew, which can spread to the fruits and cause them to split. It's caused by dry soil and humid air around the plant, so prevent it by soaking the soil well and, where possible, not getting water on the top growth. Remove the affected leaves as soon as you see them and, ideally, burn them.

Pumpkins In exceptionally dry weather, water well – 11 litres (2.2 gallons) a week for each one, and for large Halloween pumpkins, add liquid fertiliser such as seaweed extract when you water.

Sweetcorn The corn should be perfect for harvesting this month. Check for ripeness, as in July.

Soft-fruit bushes

Blackcurrants, gooseberries and redcurrants Keep the cage free of weeds and make sure the plants don't dry out.

Raspberries Although you have picked the flowers on the summer-fruiting varieties to prevent the canes bearing fruit during the first year, in subsequent years there will be plenty of fruit. When that time comes, the canes that have carried the crop need to be cut down as close to ground level as possible as soon as fruiting is over. You need a pair of sharp secateurs to make a clean cut, otherwise a jagged stub can allow pests and diseases to enter.

Spread a thick mulch along the row over the stubs, which will help them to rot away completely. Tie in new canes that have been produced during the summer to the wires with soft twine to give you one cane every 10cm (4in). If there are more than this, prune those out, too.

Harvest berries of autumn-fruiting varieties as they ripen. Once the canes are well established in the second year, you can prune out a few fruited canes to encourage more growth and extend the fruiting season. But, as a general rule, autumn-fruiting raspberries aren't pruned until late winter.

On the turn
When the silky tassels turn brown, the corn cobs are ready to harvest

Soft fruit in pots

Blueberries Carry on picking berries if there are any, although, obviously, there will be much more fruit in future years. Make sure the compost never dries out – using rain water, if possible, but if you have no choice, check that the plants don't show signs of chlorosis (see page 75).

Strawberries Harvest strawberries such as Mara des Bois and any others that are still cropping. When the latter plants have finished, cut off the old leaves as close to the central crown as possible. This enables the plants to produce new leaves to take them through the winter. The exception is Mara des Bois, a 'perpetual' variety, which carries on fruiting intermittently until autumn and so needs to keep its leaves. Make sure that the runners you have potted up don't dry out.

Fruit trees

Apricots, figs and peaches Pick as the last fruits ripen.

Flowers

Convolvulus tricolor, cornflowers, love-in-a-mist (Nigella), California and Shirley poppies, pot marigold (Calendula) and the bishop's flower (Ammi majus) Carry on picking. To keep plants producing, check them regularly for seedheads and remove them. Towards the end of the month, leave a few dead flowers to develop into seedheads for seeds next year.

In the greenhouse
Fruiting vegetables

Aubergines These should be swelling nicely. Remove all but four or five fruits and all subsequent flowers to allow those that remain to reach a decent size.

Chillies Red chillies are hotter than green ones so harvest them before they turn red if you prefer them milder.

Cucumbers Continue to harvest as they are ready.

Sweet peppers Pick green peppers or harvest when they ripen further and turn red.

Tomatoes These should be cropping heavily. As you harvest from the bottom upwards, remove the leaves below the ripening trusses of fruit. This enables the sun to reach the fruits. Don't remove any leaves above the trusses, as that will interfere with ripening.

August

Spiced Pickled Runner Beans

Makes about 6 x 350ml (1lb) jars

This recipe was given to me by Kathleen Field from Bungay in Suffolk, and was first published in the *Food Aid Cookbook* in 1986. She said then, 'There comes a time in late summer when the family say, "Oh, not runner beans again". Well, they must be picked, and here's what to do with them.' We've been doing just that with ours each year since then and the chutney is now a firm favourite. Thanks, Kathleen!

900g (2lb) runner beans
(weight after trimming and slicing)

700g (1lb 8oz) onions, chopped

850ml (1½ pints) malt vinegar

40g (1½oz) cornflour

1 heaped tablespoon mustard powder

1 rounded tablespoon turmeric

225g (8oz) soft brown sugar

450g (1lb) demerara sugar

salt

You will also need a preserving pan and 6 x 350ml (1lb) jars.

First of all, put the chopped onions into a preserving pan (or large casserole or saucepan) with 275ml (10fl oz) of the malt vinegar. Bring them up to simmering point and let them simmer gently for about 20 minutes or until the onions are soft.

Meanwhile, cook the sliced runner beans in boiling, salted water for 5 minutes, then strain them in a colander and add to the onions in the preserving (or other) pan.

Now in a small basin mix together the cornflour, mustard powder and turmeric with a little of the remaining vinegar – enough to make a smooth paste – then add this paste to the runner bean and onion mixture.

Next, pour in the rest of the malt vinegar and simmer everything for 10 minutes. After that, stir in both quantities of soft brown and demerara sugar until they dissolve and continue to simmer everything for a further 15 minutes.

Meanwhile, to sterilise the jars, wash them thoroughly in warm soapy water, rinse and heat in a moderate oven for about 5 minutes.

Finally, pot the pickled runner beans in the warmed, sterilised jars, and seal and label them when cold.

Keep the pickle for at least a month before eating.

Roasted Tomato and Goats' Cheese Tart with Thyme

Serves 6

I always make masses of fresh tomato and basil sauce and lots of gazpacho in the summer, which only tastes good when the tomatoes are very red and ripe. Once you've made this tart, I guarantee you will go on making it because it's just about the easiest and most sublime tomato recipe on record.

740g (1lb 10oz) red, ripe tomatoes
150g (5oz) soft goats' cheese
4 teaspoons chopped fresh thyme, plus a few small sprigs
1 x 375g pack fresh, ready-rolled puff pastry
2 cloves garlic, crushed
2 tablespoons extra virgin olive oil
salt and freshly milled black pepper

You will also need a large baking sheet, lightly oiled.

Pre-heat the oven to gas mark 5, 190°C (375°F).

To begin the recipe, first of all, unwrap the pastry and then place it on the baking sheet. Then, using a sharp knife, carefully score a line on the pastry, about 1cm (½in) in from the edge, all the way around but be careful not to cut it all the way through.

Now tip the goats' cheese into a small bowl, add the crushed garlic, the chopped thyme and a good seasoning of salt and freshly milled black pepper.

Then give it all a good mixing and, using a small palette or other round-bladed knife, carefully spread the cheese mixture evenly all over the surface of the pastry, right up to the line.

Next, thinly slice all the tomatoes (no need to peel them) and arrange them on top of the cheese in overlapping lines lengthways; overlap one line one way and the other next to it the other way.

After that, season the tomatoes and then drizzle the olive oil and scatter the sprigs of thyme all over them.

Bake on a middle shelf for 55 minutes or until the pastry is golden brown and the tomatoes are roasted and slightly charred at the edges.

To serve the tart warm, leave it to settle for about 10 minutes before cutting into squares.

Piedmont Roasted Peppers

Serves 4 as a starter

This recipe is quite simply stunning: hard to imagine how something so easily prepared can taste so good. Its history is colourful, too. It was first discovered by Elizabeth David and published in her splendid book *Italian Food*.

4 large red peppers (green are not suitable)
4 medium tomatoes
8 tinned anchovy fillets, drained
2 cloves garlic
8 dessertspoons Italian extra virgin olive oil
freshly milled black pepper
a small bunch of fresh basil leaves, to serve

You will also need a good, solid, shallow roasting tray, 30 x 40cm (12 x 16in). If the sides are too deep, the roasted vegetables won't get those lovely, nutty, toasted edges.

Pre-heat the oven to gas mark 4, 180°C (350°F).

Begin by cutting the peppers in half and removing the seeds but leaving the stalks intact (they're not edible but they do look attractive and they help the pepper halves to keep their shape). Lay the pepper halves in the lightly oiled roasting tray. Now put the tomatoes in a bowl and pour boiling water over them. Leave them for 1 minute, then drain them and slip the skins off, using a cloth to protect your hands. Then cut the tomatoes into quarters and place 2 quarters in each pepper half.

After that, snip one anchovy fillet per pepper half into rough pieces and add to the tomatoes. Peel the garlic cloves, slice them thinly and divide the slices equally among the tomatoes and anchovies. Now spoon 1 dessertspoon of olive oil into each pepper, season with freshly milled pepper (but no salt because of the anchovies) and place the tray on a high shelf in the oven for the peppers to roast for 50 minutes to 1 hour.

Then transfer the cooked peppers to a serving dish, with all the precious juices poured over, and garnish with a few scattered basil leaves. These do need good bread to go with them as the juices are sublime – focaccia would be perfect.

Autumn

September

Summer may be over, but there is much to relish and still time to sow winter varieties

TASKS FOR SEPTEMBER

Collect seedheads from flowers

Harvest aubergines, beetroot, blueberries, borlotti beans, Brussels sprouts, cabbages, carrots, cauliflowers, chard, chillies, courgettes, cucumbers, dwarf French beans, herbs, leeks, lettuces, pak choi, parsnips, potatoes, radishes, raspberries, red cabbage, rocket, runner beans, spinach, spinach beet, strawberries, sweetcorn, sweet peppers, tomatoes, turnips

Plant cabbages, herbs, strawberries

Protect cabbages, rocket, salad leaves

Sow autumn/winter salad mix, green crop manure, herbs, lettuces, radishes, rocket, spinach, spring onions, turnips

September sees the start of autumn and, although the days can still be warm or even hot, the nights are beginning to draw in and are definitely cooler. Some colder places may see early night frosts. The kitchen garden is still very productive, although many crops are coming to an end now – the dwarf French beans, for example, as well as the borlotti and runner beans. Looking ahead to the winter and early spring, there's time to sow more salads and oriental greens.

In the garden

Beans

Borlotti beans The pods will be a really bright red now. Harvest the last of the beans. If you are saving some to dry, leave them on the plant until the pods are hard and the contents rattle when you shake them. Then shell the beans, let them dry thoroughly and store them in an airtight jar or tin in a cool, dry, dark place. Similarly, if you want to save some of the beans to sow as seed next year, treat them in the same way.

When they finish cropping, clear the plants by cutting them off at soil level. Don't dig out the plants, roots and all, because the nodules on the roots are valuable for incorporating nitrogen in the soil. This will be of great benefit to leafy brassicas that can follow the beans in this bed next season.

Dwarf French beans Harvest the last of the dwarf French beans now and clear in the same way as the borlotti beans.

Runner beans Enjoy the last of the crops this month. At the end of September, cut all the plants down to just above soil level, then pull out the poles, untangle the bean plants from them and put the plants in the compost bin. Store the poles for next year in the garden shed, if you have one, or in the garage.

It's a snip Cutting off runner beans at soil level

Continuous cycle
Far left When the runner beans have finished, untangle the bean plants and pull out the poles

Left Seedlings on their way for next spring

Brassicas and leafy greens

Brussels sprouts Early varieties of sprouts should be ready for harvesting now. Small sprouts are best – full of flavour and not as bitter as the older ones. Pick them from the bottom of the stalk upwards by snapping them off with a downward flick of the wrist. Remove any yellowing leaves, along with any sprouts that have 'blown' – opened out – and are like mini cabbages rather than tight, hard buttons. If your vegetable plot is a long way from the house, you can cut a whole stem (or 'tree'), stand it in a cool place in just 5cm (2in) of water in a bucket and harvest your sprouts fresh, as required.

For overwintering, especially in windy gardens, earthing up (drawing soil around) the stems of the sprouts helps to support them.

Cabbages Continue to plant out seedlings for next spring. It's worth protecting cabbage seedlings with horticultural fleece now to deter pests and protect the crops from the cold.

Although the cabbage root fly is less active at this time of year, females can still lay the eggs that turn into grubs and attack the roots

in a mild autumn, or they may survive the winter and do the same in the spring. Horticultural fleece will also deter the pigeons, which can pull the seedlings out or strip the leaves. Harvest the last of any summer red cabbages.

Cauliflowers Carry on harvesting.

Chard As this grows, eat it as baby leaves or let it grow on.

Spinach Depending on the weather, you may already have a crop of baby leaves from last month's sowing ready to be picked now. Either way, sow some more spinach for next spring.

Spinach beet This might be ready for picking as a cut-and-come-again crop towards the end of the month. Otherwise, you can leave it to grow on to eat like spinach.

Bulbs, roots and stems

Asparagus As soon as all the fern has turned brown, cut it off at soil level. This will stop it being rocked by autumn gales and damaging the crowns. It's a good idea to mulch the ridges by covering them with 5cm (2in) of coarse organic matter to stop the soil from being compacted by heavy rain in autumn and winter.

Beetroot Carry on harvesting.

Carrots Pull the last of the maincrop carrots to prevent slug damage. You can store them in boxes or trays of damp sand or compost in a dry place.

Celery Continue to check that there are no pests such as slugs or snails inside the plastic pipes that are blanching the stems.

Leeks Carry on harvesting. If you live in a very cold area, it is worth filling a bucket with compost and digging up 10-12 leeks, depending on the size, and putting them in the bucket. Stand the bucket in a shed or by a wall. This way, even if the ground freezes, you will still be able to enjoy your leeks fresh.

Parsnips The roots will be ready now, but remember, for sweeter parsnips, wait until there has been a frost before harvesting.

Potatoes Harvest the Belle de Fontenay and the last of the Pink Fir Apple. Clear away the top growth and put on the compost heap, making sure there are no tubers left in the ground. In Delia's garden, as part of the crop rotation plan, peas and beans were grown in these beds the next season.

The maincrop potato Desirée will be ready for harvesting. You can leave them in the ground for a few weeks longer, taking them out as you need them, or, if slugs are a problem, harvest them all and store in brown paper sacks in a cool, dark place. Either way, once they have all been lifted, clear the ground completely. It's well worth sowing green manure in the bed now (see page 16).

Radishes Carry on picking and sow another part-row.

You could sow winter radishes. These are more like turnips than the summer kinds, and can be eaten raw when small, or left to grow on, then cooked. The leaves may be added to stir-fries. Look for Munchen Bier or the Black Spanish Round or varieties of the tapering white Japanese mouli, such as Minowase, or April Cross F1.

Spring onions Sow another part-row or two of a winter-hardy variety for early crops next spring.

Turnips Harvest any remaining turnips. You could sow a very quick-growing variety such as Tokyo Cross F1 now. They will be ready in just over a month if the weather is mild.

Oriental greens

Mizuna If your mizuna seedlings were not large enough to thin last month, do so this month.

Mustard spinach Treat this as mizuna.

Pak choi Harvest this as a cut-and-come-again crop, or leave to grow on to full size.

You can sow more of all these oriental greens, if you like, to enjoy over the coming months.

Salad leaves

Lettuces Carry on harvesting. You can still sow the hardier varieties such as All The Year Round this month but, unless we have a very long, mild autumn, you are unlikely to get a crop from these sowings before the spring now. In cold areas protect sowings with a cloche from the end of the month onwards. In warmer, more sheltered gardens, lettuces won't need protection until later in October.

Or, you could sow an autumn/winter salad mix. There are various combinations available – English, French and Italian – as well as some mixes that include non-lettuce leaves, such as claytonia (winter purslane), leaf radish and lambs' lettuce. Some also contain a selection of oriental leaves. Cover sowings with a cloche in late autumn/early winter.

Radicchio Thin the seedlings, if you have not already done so, and in very dry weather water well.

Rocket Continue to pick. Sow another part-row and, with some protection such as cloches from the end of the month onwards, it should survive the winter.

Squash and sweetcorn

Courgettes The plants will be more or less exhausted, so harvest the last courgettes. Then dig up the plants, chop them up with a spade and put them in the compost bin.

It's well worth sowing a green manure crop in the empty bed over the winter (see page 16).

Pumpkins The pumpkins will be swelling now but they should take care of themselves because their trailing growths root as they go to find water. However, in periods of real drought, give them a thorough watering every week.

Sweetcorn Finish harvesting, then dig up the plants and chop them with a spade before putting them in the compost bin.

DELIA IN THE KITCHEN Leeks

To prepare leeks, first take off the tough outer leaves and trim off most of the very green part. Now, using a sharp knife, place the leek on a flat surface and make an incision vertically about halfway down (because of the intricate layers, there can be dust and grit trapped in between, usually in the upper part). Now turn on the cold tap and fan out the layers of leek to rinse them through and rid them of any hidden dirt. When the leeks are trimmed and washed, cut them all the way through vertically, then chop them into 2.5cm (1in) pieces ∎

Top left The pumpkin emerges – its trailing stems put down roots to seek water

Top right Dusky pink Desirée potatoes

Below left Growing basil in a pot

Below right Storing leeks in compost in a bucket is a good idea if you live in a cold area

Strawberry bed

Far right Planting a runner in a strawberry bed, through weed-suppressing MyPex

Right When the last of the strawberries are done, remove the plants and, if you've been growing your runners on, you can plant them now. Re-fill the pots with fresh compost first

Soft-fruit bushes

Blackcurrants, gooseberries and redcurrants Keep the weeds at bay and water the bushes if there isn't much rain.

Raspberries Harvest the Autumn Bliss raspberries as they continue to turn red and ripen.

Soft fruit in pots

Blueberries Make sure that they don't dry out. Harvest any late-ripening berries.

Strawberries Even a perpetual variety such as Mara des Bois will finish cropping this month. Unlike non-perpetual fruiting varieties, these should not have their old leaves removed once fruiting is finished. You can leave the plants in pots outside for next year.

Alternatively, you can plant the strawberries out into the ground, then clean the pots, re-fill them with compost and re-plant them with runners you have been growing on. The strawberry plants from the pots in Delia's garden were planted in a narrow bed around the perimeter of the fruit cage.

Strawberries need well-prepared soil that is fertile and free draining, which may mean adding both bulky organic matter and grit if the soil in your garden is heavy. Before planting, lay weed-suppressing membrane, such as MyPex, over the prepared soil and then cut 'X's in the membrane, through which the strawberries should be planted.

If you are leaving the original plants in the pots, plant any runners you have potted up 30cm (12in) apart in a strawberry bed, or, if you have no space, give them away.

If you are starting from scratch, you can buy bare-rooted strawberry plants now. Plant them 30cm (12in) apart and in holes deep enough to take the roots well spread out. If necessary, you can trim any extra-long roots to about 10cm (4in). Firm the soil around the roots and water well to make sure there are no air pockets.

Herbs

Basil, chervil, chives, coriander, mint, parsley, rosemary, sage, tarragon, thyme Keep picking herbs as you need them. You'll have sage, rosemary and thyme all through the winter but the other herbs outside will begin to fade towards the end of September and into October.

For a guaranteed supply of other fresh herbs, you can also freeze some, such as parsley, now, either washed and placed whole in freezer bags, or chopped, put in ice-cube trays, covered with water, then frozen that way. Store the resulting cubes in bags. Some herbs – chives and mint – are worth transferring to pots to keep inside over the winter (see page 111).

Flowers

Convolvulus tricolor, cornflowers, love-in-a-mist (Nigella), California and Shirley poppies, pot marigold (Calendula) and the bishop's flower (Ammi majus) All the annuals will be more or less spent by now, although you may still have a few flowers appearing here and there. In Delia's kitchen garden the California poppies carried on flowering profusely right through September and October! Incidentally, this is a good time to collect seed from all the annuals for next year. Collect the seedheads on a dry day.

California poppies have long, narrow, curving seedheads. When the seed is ripe the pods turn pale golden brown and split. If you are in luck, they will just have started splitting when you collect them, so all you need to do is open the pod fully and brush out the seeds inside with your finger.

Shirley poppies have seedheads like miniature salt shakers. Turn them carefully upside down over a clean sheet of white paper and shake gently. Hundreds of tiny black seeds should come out. Leave them to dry out thoroughly.

Love-in-a-mist also has large, round seed pods, each one containing dozens of larger black seeds.

Store seeds during the winter months in plastic film canisters or envelopes placed in an airtight plastic food container in the salad drawer of the fridge. Make sure that each variety is clearly labelled.

Ripe and ready
Far left In the greenhouse, keep picking cucumbers as they are ready

Left The sweet peppers gradually turn from green to vivid red – use in salads, stir-fries or roast them

In the greenhouse
Fruiting vegetables

Aubergines As the fruits turn a rich, deep, glossy purple colour, cut the stems about 2.5cm (1in) above the calyx – the green junction of stem and fruit.

Chillies Pick these as they turn red. Use them fresh or dry them for winter either by picking the ripe fruits and leaving them in a cool, dry place until they are dry, or by lifting the whole plant and hanging it upside down to dry. You can also pickle them in vinegar.

Cucumbers Keep harvesting them before they are too large.

Sweet peppers Harvest the later fruits as they turn red. Keep them well watered and fed with tomato fertiliser once a week.

Tomatoes Carry on harvesting. Keep them well watered and give them fertiliser every week.

Herbs
Chives, coriander, mint, parsley You can keep some herbs, such as chives or mint, going through the winter if you plant them in pots and stand them in a frost-free, but cool place inside – a porch, an unheated conservatory, or in the greenhouse. You'll need a few 30cm (12in) pots and a soil-based compost. Herbs need well-drained compost so either mix a handful or two of fine grit into a soil-based compost such as John Innes No 3 or a 50:50 mixture of multipurpose compost and soil-based compost. Machine-made terracotta pots are very good value, but do look rather raw. To age them, see page 22.

If you have chives in the garden, dig up a clump now and pull off a decent-size piece from the outside, re-planting the rest in the soil. Trim any dead leaves and stems and plant it in a pot.

To re-plant mint, cut a few pieces of root, with shoots, from the outside of the patch, and plant them in another pot.

You can sow coriander and parsley inside now in pots for autumn and winter supplies. Sow thinly in drills 15cm (6in) apart.

DELIA IN THE KITCHEN Chillies

How to prepare chillies – very carefully. Why? Because the membrane and the seeds inside are the hottest part and can burn delicate skin. American cookbooks often advise using rubber gloves, but washing your hands with soap and water after handling should be okay. What happens is, if your hands touch the delicate skin on your face or, worse, eyes, it can burn the skin. So slice the tops off, cut them in half lengthways, hold down the tip of each chilli half with your finger and, using a sharp knife, scrape away all the membrane and seeds and discard them. After that, either slice the chilli or chop it finely, then carefully wash your hands ■

September

Oven-baked Smoked Pancetta and Leek Risotto

Serves 6 as a starter or 4 as a main course

This oven-baked risotto is made with leeks and smoked pancetta and, of course, lots of lovely melting cheese.

110g (4oz) sliced smoked pancetta

350g (12oz) leeks, trimmed, halved,

rinsed and sliced (trimmed weight should be about 225g/8oz)

175ml (6fl oz) Italian carnaroli rice

60g (2½oz) butter

1 small onion, finely chopped

75ml (3fl oz) dry white wine

510ml (18fl oz) hot vegetable stock

1 dessertspoon chopped fresh sage

½ teaspoon salt

2 tablespoons Pecorino Romano cheese, freshly grated,

plus 50g (2oz) to serve

freshly milled black pepper

You will also need a 5cm (2in) deep, ovenproof baking dish, 23cm (9in) square.

Pre-heat the oven to gas mark 2, 150°C (300°F).

Begin by reserving 5 slices of pancetta, then cut the rest into thin strips. Melt the butter in a medium saucepan, add the strips of pancetta to the pan, along with the onion, and let them cook over a gentle heat for 5-7 minutes, until the onion is soft and golden.

Meanwhile, place the baking dish in the oven to warm through. Now add the leeks and the rice to the saucepan, stirring them around to get a good coating of butter (it will look like there's not nearly enough rice at this stage, but it swells up during cooking), then add the white wine and vegetable stock. Next, add the sage, half a teaspoon of salt and some freshly milled black pepper and bring it up to simmering point, then transfer the whole lot from the pan to the warmed dish. Stir once, then place it on the centre shelf of the oven (without covering) to cook for exactly 20 minutes – a timer is useful here.

Meanwhile, pre-heat the grill to its highest setting for 10 minutes or so, then place the 5 reserved slices of pancetta on a piece of foil and grill them 7.5cm (3in) from the heat for about 5 minutes: it's important to get them really crisp. When they're cool enough to handle, crumble into tiny pieces and leave to one side. After the 20 minutes are up, slide the dish out along the oven shelf and gently stir in the 2 tablespoons of grated Pecorino, turning the rice grains over. Now put the timer on again and cook the risotto for a further 15 minutes, then remove from the oven and put a clean tea towel over it while you invite everyone to sit down. Serve on warmed plates and sprinkle with the crispy pancetta and the extra grated Pecorino.

Tunisian Aubergine Salad with Coriander and Yoghurt

Serves 4 as a starter

This is my adaptation of an Elizabeth David recipe. I never actually made it from her book, but one of my favourite restaurants, Chez Bruce, in Wandsworth, London, regularly serves it as a first course. It's so wonderful I never have anything else if it's on the menu.

700g (1lb 8oz) aubergine,
chopped into 1cm (½in) cubes
2 rounded tablespoons chopped fresh coriander
700g (1lb 8oz) ripe, red tomatoes
3-4 tablespoons olive oil
1 heaped teaspoon cumin seeds
1 teaspoon allspice berries
1 large onion (weighing about 275g/10oz),
finely chopped
1 large red chilli, deseeded and finely chopped
4 cloves garlic, finely chopped
2 rounded tablespoons chopped fresh mint
salt and freshly milled black pepper

To serve
4 tablespoons Greek yoghurt
8 pitta breads, warmed
1 tablespoon olive oil
1 rounded tablespoon chopped fresh coriander
1 rounded tablespoon chopped fresh mint

You will also need 2 large baking trays, one 28 x 40cm (11 x 16in), the other 25.5 x 35cm (10 x 14in).

You'll need to start this recipe the day before you want to serve it. First of all, salt and drain the aubergines. To do this, place them in a large colander and, as you add them to the colander, sprinkle with 1 tablespoon of salt. Then cover with a plate and weigh it down with a few scale weights or a similarly heavy object.

Now place the colander on a plate and leave the chopped aubergine to drain for 1 hour. When it has been draining for 30 minutes, pre-heat the oven to gas mark 8, 230°C (450°F).

Meanwhile, skin the tomatoes. To do this, pour boiling water over them and leave for exactly 1 minute or, if the tomatoes are small, 15-30 seconds, before draining them and slipping off their skins (protecting your hands with a cloth if they are too hot). Cut the skinned tomatoes in half and place them, cut-side up, on the smaller baking tray, which should be lightly oiled, and brush the tomatoes with a little olive oil as well. Set to one side.

Now you need to dry-roast the cumin seeds and allspice berries, and to do this place them in a small frying pan or saucepan over a medium heat and stir and toss them around for 1-2 minutes, or until they begin to look toasted and start to jump in the pan. Now transfer them to a pestle and mortar and crush them to a powder.

When the aubergines are ready, squeeze them to get rid of any excess juices, dry them in a clean tea cloth, then place them in a bowl. Add 1 tablespoon of the olive oil and toss the cubes of aubergine around so they get a good coating.

After that, spread them out on the larger baking tray and place both baking trays in the oven, with the aubergines on the top shelf and the tomatoes on the next one down. Give them about 25 minutes, by which time the aubergines should be tinged golden brown at the edges and the tomatoes soft. Remove the vegetables from the oven and, when the tomatoes are cool enough, chop them into small pieces.

Meanwhile, heat 2 more tablespoons of the oil in a large frying pan over a medium to high heat and fry the onions until soft and pale gold – about 5 minutes – then add the chilli and garlic and fry for 1 more minute.

Next, add the chopped tomatoes, aubergines and crushed spices, stir well, add the herbs and season with salt and freshly milled black pepper.

Bring everything up to a gentle simmer, then remove the pan from the heat and pile everything into a serving dish. Leave for 24 hours, or longer if possible, covered in the fridge. Serve the aubergine salad at room temperature, drizzled with the tablespoon of olive oil.

Serve with the warm pitta breads, about a tablespoon of Greek yoghurt with each serving and the fresh, chopped coriander and mint scattered over.

October

The leaves are turning and it's a season of change with autumn produce ready to harvest

TASKS FOR OCTOBER

Clean the greenhouse

Dig next year's runner-bean trench

Harvest aubergines, beetroot, Brussels sprouts, cabbages, carrots, cauliflowers, celery, chard, chillies, cucumbers, leeks, mizuna, mustard spinach, pak choi, parsnips, pumpkins, raspberries, rocket, spinach, spinach beet, sweet peppers, tomatoes

Plant rhubarb

Protect autumn/winter salad mix, broad beans, lettuces, peas, radicchio, rocket, spinach, spinach beet, spring onions

Sow broad beans, garlic, peas

It's a time of change in the vegetable garden, with many crops now over and the winter vegetables coming into their own – the leeks and parsnips, celery and Brussels sprouts will all taste better if there are hard frosts that turn some of the starch to sugar. It's also a time to look forward to the next season, with some crops being planted or sown now, under protection, to crop early in the spring. At the beginning of the month there is still enough warmth in the soil for seeds to germinate and start growing before the shorter days and lower temperatures bring almost all growth to a halt for the winter.

In the garden

Beans and peas

Broad beans Sow early in the month, as in March (see page 30) in single or double rows.

Peas Sow a double row, in a flat-bottomed trench as in the spring (see page 30).

Sow beans and peas in their new beds in the kitchen garden (where potatoes were grown in the previous season) to rotate the crops. The soil in which you are sowing them will still be warm from the summer sunshine but cover the newly sown crops with an extra wide (1m/3ft 3in), polythene tunnel cloche to protect them from the forthcoming winter.

Runner-bean trench Dig a trench for next summer's runner beans, as in March (see page 30), and start putting kitchen waste into it – fruit and vegetable peelings and so on.

Brassicas and leafy greens

Brussels sprouts Carry on picking sprouts while they are small directly from the plant or from a whole stem or 'tree' that you have cut and stored to harvest from.

Cabbages Harvest the first late autumn/winter cabbages now, including later varieties of red cabbage. Keep the cabbages protected with horticultural fleece to ward off pests and the worst of the cold weather, particularly if there is risk of frost.

Pumpkin pride Glorious orange globes – if the skin is firm and they sound hollow when you give them a tap, they're ready

Cauliflowers You should be able to carry on harvesting these for a month or so, depending on how many you sowed.

Chard Continue to pick as you wish.

Spinach Some of the crop may be large enough to harvest as baby leaves. Protect growing plants with cloches at the end of the month for a very early crop next year.

Spinach beet Pick this as you need it through the month. It won't put on a great deal more growth after the end of October. Although it is hardy enough to come through all but the coldest weather, unprotected, the leaves can get a bit battered, so cover with a cloche, as for spinach.

Bulbs, roots and stems

Beetroot Harvest the last of the beetroot.

Carrots If you sowed a late variety in July, you should be able to start harvesting them now.

Celery Carry on checking, from time to time, that the celery remains pest free. After the first hard frost, harvest the heads as you need them. To do this, dig up the plant, remove the collar (pipe) and trim off the longer roots. If the weather has been unseasonably dry, water well before you harvest, to prevent the stalks from wilting.

Garlic Now is a good time to sow garlic, which will be ready for harvesting early next summer. Although we think of garlic as a Mediterranean plant, it actually needs a period of cold weather to get it going. It's best to buy special seed garlic to sow, rather than the kind you normally get in the shops for cooking, as it is certified free from disease. The Italian red variety Rosso di Saluggia that was used in Delia's garden is from the north of Italy and so is accustomed to cold weather.

To sow, break up the heads of garlic into separate cloves and remove any loose, papery skin, taking care not to damage the base plate (the flat bit at the opposite end to the tip). Plant the cloves in rows 25.5-30cm (10–12in) apart, about 7.5-10cm (3-4in) deep and with 15cm (6in) between them, pointed end uppermost. If your garden has very heavy, wet soil, which could cause the cloves to rot, it's best to start them off in modules, and keep them in a cool, frost-free place over the winter, then plant them out in the spring once they have sprouted.

If you are a garlic lover, you can sow cloves through the winter months, as late as March, for harvesting next September – unless the soil is waterlogged or frozen. Harvested garlic can be plaited and hung to dry in a cool, dry place (see page 130).

Leeks Carry on harvesting the leeks. In colder areas, you can still store some in compost in a bucket.

Parsnips Harvest, as required. You can leave the parsnips in the ground, but if you have had problems with carrot fly in the past, harvest now and store them in wooden boxes of damp sand or compost in a cool, dark place.

Radishes The summer radishes will be finishing at this stage, and the winter ones won't be ready yet.

Spring onions Crops sown this month will benefit from protection with cloches in very cold weather. They can be left until they crop early next spring.

Turnips If you sowed a quick-growing variety in September and the weather has been mild, check to see if they're ready.

Oriental greens

Mizuna, mustard spinach and pak choi Continue to harvest these as cut-and-come-again or full-size crops.

Salad leaves

Lettuces Protect hardier varieties sown for the spring with a cloche from the end of this month. Otherwise, they will need little attention.

If you sowed an autumn/winter salad mix, this will also benefit from covering and you should be able to enjoy eating the leaves soon.

Radicchio This will need the protection of a cloche now – in Delia's garden we used a tent cloche – or you could use a double layer of horticultural fleece.

Rocket Harvest leaves, as required, from under the cloches.

Feel the benefit
In colder weather, radicchio needs protecting. This tent cloche is made from two panels of polyurethene clipped at the top

Autumn/winter carrots: My favourite way to cook them plainly is to scrape off the skins and cut them into 5cm (2in) chunks, then place them in a saucepan with salt and enough boiling water to barely cover them. Give them about 20 minutes, or until tender but with a little firm bite in the centre, then drain and place them in a food processor and, using the pulse movement, 'chop' the carrots quite small, but don't overdo it or you'll have a purée. Quickly return them to the saucepan using a spatula to scrape them back in quickly, add a knob of butter and some freshly milled black pepper, then place them over a gentle heat and stir them around for a couple of minutes to get the heat back in. 450g (1lb) of carrots will serve 4 ▪

Squash

Pumpkins If the fruits are a glorious orange colour and have a hard skin and sound hollow when you tap them, they are ready to harvest, to cook or to carve into lanterns.

Once all the pumpkins have been cut, remove the plants, chop them up with a spade and add them to the compost bin.

Fruit bed

Strawberries If the weather is dry, make sure you water planted-out strawberries to help them get established before the really cold weather sets in.

Soft-fruit bushes

Blackcurrants, gooseberries, redcurrants Make sure they don't dry out if there has been no rain. If there is bare soil at the base of the gooseberry bushes, go over the surface lightly with a hoe to expose sawfly larvae to the frost that will kill them.

Raspberries Harvest the last few berries of autumn-fruiting varieties. These canes are pruned during late winter.

Soft fruit in pots

Blueberries As these lose their leaves (they are deciduous, shedding their leaves annually at the end of the growing season), they will need less water but in a very dry autumn/winter make sure the compost does not dry out completely.

Strawberries Make sure the plants or runners planted last month don't go short of water through the colder months.

Other fruit

Rhubarb Although associated mainly with sweet dishes, rhubarb is technically a vegetable not a fruit as it is the stalks we eat (beware – the leaves are poisonous). You can grow it from seed, but it isn't always successful. So it's best to buy plants or crowns, as they are called, from a garden centre or nursery. Rhubarb likes soil that is

DELIA IN THE KITCHEN Pumpkins

To prepare pumpkin, you need a good, sharp, heavy knife, and first you cut the vegetable in half and then into quarters. After that, scoop out the fibrous bits and all the seeds with a spoon or knife, then, this time, using a small but very sharp knife, peel away the tough skin. Finally, cut the pumpkin flesh into cubes or slices. The smooth, silky texture makes wonderful soup, and gives the best texture in pumpkin pie ■

Spaced out

Far right A pot of parsley seedlings. For a supply through the winter months, thin first to 5cm (2in), then 10cm (4in) apart

Right You'll get a better result if you plant rhubarb from plants rather than seed, giving each one plenty of growing space – 1m (3ft 3in) per plant

fertile and fairly heavy but not waterlogged. Each plant needs plenty of space because the leaves are so large. If you are planting more than one plant in a bed, allow about 1m (3ft 3in) per plant either way. Plant the rhubarb so that the crown is just below soil level.

Mulch the soil around it with well-rotted manure or garden compost to conserve moisture and keep weeds at bay but don't cover the crown itself or it may rot. To let the plants get established, don't pull any sticks in the first year. In later years, you can force it to crop in late March or April by covering it with a terracotta rhubarb forcer or even a bucket in mid-winter, once the first signs of growth appear. Harvest unforced rhubarb from May, leaving at least half the stems on each plant to keep it actively growing and producing.

DELIA IN THE KITCHEN Aubergines

Chefs and cooks seem to have an endless debate about aubergines – to salt and drain or not to salt and drain. I'm for the former. I do take the point that the modern aubergine has evolved to a state where it does not contain bitter juices, but the juices are there nonetheless and I find salting and draining gets rid of excess moisture and concentrates the flavour – there's nothing worse than a watery aubergine. Aubergines also have a capacity to absorb other flavours, so are great mixed with tomatoes and spices, cheese or pulses. They also absorb oil at an incredible rate, so frying is not recommended. I find the best way to cook them is either by oven-roasting or char-grilling ■

In the greenhouse

Fruiting vegetables

Aubergines, sweet peppers Harvest the last of the aubergines and sweet peppers, remove the plants and take them to the compost bin and clean the pots.

Chillies Pick the last of them or, if there are still lots of unripe fruits on the plant, remove it from the pot and hang it upside down in a warm place indoors to let the fruit ripen.

Cucumbers Harvest the last of the fruits, then untangle the vine from its supports and remove the plant from the growing bag. Chop up the plant and put it in the compost bin. If you like, you can top up the growing bag with fresh compost and re-use it to sow a mix of autumn/winter salad leaves.

Tomatoes Carry on picking ripe tomatoes. In an unheated greenhouse, green tomatoes may ripen slowly if the weather isn't too cold. If it is, or you need the space, pick the green tomatoes and put them in a warm place to ripen, or pull up the entire plant, shake off the compost and hang it upside down somewhere warm. If there are lots of green tomatoes, use them for chutney. Clean the pots.

Autumn cleaning
Far left On a mild day, you can pop any plants left in the greenhouse outside while you scrub down the structure, the benches and the glass, inside and out

Left Use the garden hose and scrub with a firm brush to make sure your garden pots are really clean

Herbs

Chives, coriander, mint, parsley If you have planted chives and mint from the garden into pots, as suggested, they should be growing well now.

Once the parsley and coriander that were sown last month have germinated, you can thin the seedlings to 5cm (2in) apart and finally, to 10cm (4in) apart. The plants should then continue to grow happily and keep you supplied with fresh herbs over the winter.

Cleaning the greenhouse

With the greenhouse almost empty and the weather still mild enough for any plants and seedlings to go outside for the day, this is a good time to clean it, to make sure that it's harbouring no pests or diseases to give you problems next year.

Take everything out, remove any shading and scrub down the structure and the benches, using a soft scrubbing brush and hot, soapy water with some horticultural disinfectant added.

Wash the glass, too, both inside and out. It is surprising how much light even slightly dirty glass can cut out, and that makes a big difference in the winter months when the days are shorter and light levels are so much lower anyway.

Scrape off any algae that have accumulated where the glass meets the frames – a plastic plant label is ideal for the job. Use your garden hose, with the jet at its most powerful to rinse everything.

When the greenhouse is dry, put any plants back inside and make sure that all your essential equipment is clean and tidy.

You'll also need to clean any terracotta pots. Once you have emptied them, scrub the pots, using a stiff brush and very hot, soapy water (a squirt of washing-up liquid helps), add horticultural disinfectant to minimise any chance of diseases or eggs of pests overwintering and causing problems with crops next year. You might find it easier to remove all traces of compost if you soak the pots in water first.

Clean any plastic pots and seed trays in the same way. When they are dry, stack and store them. You can leave pots dirty over the winter, but it's so much nicer having them all ready to go when you are full of enthusiasm to start sowing in earnest next spring.

October

Green Tomato Chutney

Makes about 8 x 350ml (1lb) jars.

Originally, I thought this was a good recipe for using up all those stubborn green tomatoes that never seemed to ripen, but now we all love this chutney so much I don't even want half my tomatoes to ripen just so I'll be able to make plenty.

1.15 kg (2lb 8oz) green tomatoes (no need to peel)

900g (2lb) onions

450g (1lb) seedless raisins

1.15kg (2lb 8oz) cooking apples

6 large cloves garlic, crushed

½ tablespoon cayenne pepper

½ tablespoon salt

2 dessertspoons ground ginger

625g (1lb 6oz) soft brown or demerara sugar

25g (1oz) pickling spice

1.75 litres (3 pints) malt vinegar

You will also need a small preserving pan, 8 x 350ml (1lb) preserving jars, string and some gauze.

Wash the tomatoes and cut them into quarters; peel the onions and quarter them, quarter and core the apples, leaving the peels on and keeping them in water to prevent browning.

Using a food processor, finely chop the tomatoes and place them in the pan. Next, chop the onions, then the raisins, followed by the apples (don't worry if they have now turned brown), adding them all to the pan.

Now add the garlic, the cayenne, salt, ginger and sugar, blending everything thoroughly. Next, tie the pickling spice in a small piece of double-thickness gauze and attach it to the handle so that it hangs down into the other ingredients.

Now pour in the vinegar, bring to simmering point, remove any scum from the surface, then let it simmer very gently for about 3½ hours without covering. Stir now and then, especially towards the end, to prevent sticking. It's ready when the vinegar has been almost absorbed, the chutney has thickened to a nice soft consistency and the spoon leaves a trail. Do be careful not to overcook, and remember it does thicken up quite a bit as it cools.

To sterilise the jars, wash, thoroughly dry and heat them in a moderate oven for 5 minutes.

Pour the hot chutney into hot jars, filling them as full as possible. Cover with waxed sealing discs and seal with a tight lid at once. Label the jars when the chutney is cold.

Cauliflower with Two Cheeses and Crème Fraîche
Serves 4

No need to make a white sauce for this one – the beauty of half-fat crème fraîche is that you can simmer it into a creamy sauce in moments. This could be an accompanying vegetable for four, it could make a main course for two served with rice, or I like it with penne pasta – England meets Italy, sort of thing!

1 medium cauliflower, separated into florets

40g (1½oz) each Parmesan and Gruyère, finely grated

 plus 1 heaped tablespoon extra Parmesan, to finish

2 heaped tablespoons half-fat crème fraîche

2 bay leaves, torn in half

a little freshly grated nutmeg

2 spring onions, very finely chopped

(including the green parts)

a pinch of cayenne pepper

salt and freshly milled black pepper

You will also need an ovenproof baking dish, 19cm (7½in) square and 5cm (2in) deep.

Pre-heat the grill to its highest setting.

First of all, place the cauliflower florets and a few of the inner leaves in a steamer with the pieces of bay leaf tucked among it. Pour in some boiling water from the kettle, add some freshly grated nutmeg and salt, then cover and steam the cauliflower till tender – about 12 minutes. After this time, test the thickest parts with a skewer to see if they are tender, then remove it to the baking dish and cover with a cloth to keep warm.

Now pour 75ml (3fl oz) of the steaming water into a saucepan, add the crème fraîche and simmer, whisking well, until it has thickened very slightly, then add the cheeses. Heat this gently for about 1 minute, whisking, until the cheeses have melted, then season the sauce to taste. Now pour the sauce over the cauliflower and scatter the spring onions and extra tablespoon of Parmesan over, then sprinkle with the cayenne. Finally, place the dish under the hot grill until the cauliflower has browned and the sauce is bubbling.

Baked Apple and Almond Pudding with Mascarpone Vanilla Cream
Serves 4-6

I think of all the apple recipes this one has proved the most popular over the years and as soon as I see the windfall apples in the autumn I know it is time to make it yet again.

450g (1lb) Bramley cooking apples,

peeled, cored and sliced

110g (4oz) ground almonds

50g (2oz) soft brown sugar

110g (4oz) butter, at room temperature

110g (4oz) golden caster sugar

2 large eggs, beaten

For the mascarpone vanilla cream

250g (9oz) mascarpone, at room temperature

1 teaspoon vanilla extract

200ml (7fl oz) fromage frais

1 rounded dessertspoon golden caster sugar

You will also need a buttered dish, approximately 850ml (1½-pint) capacity.

Pre-heat the oven to gas mark 4, 180°C (350°F).

First of all, place the cooking apples in a saucepan with the soft brown sugar and approximately 1 tablespoon water. Simmer the apples and sugar gently until soft, and then arrange them in the bottom of the prepared dish.

Meanwhile, in a mixing bowl, cream together the butter and golden caster sugar until pale and fluffy and then beat in the eggs a little at a time. When all of the egg is in, next carefully and lightly fold in the ground almonds. Now spread this creamed mixture over the apples, and even out the surface with the back of a tablespoon. Then bake on a 'highish' shelf in the oven for exactly 1 hour. Meanwhile, mix together all the ingredients for the mascarpone vanilla cream until smooth, and chill until needed.

This pudding is equally good warm or cold. It will keep in the fridge for 3 or 4 days. Serve with the mascarpone vanilla cream.

November

Hearty root vegetables abound, and outside crops need protection, if frost is likely

TASKS FOR NOVEMBER

Harvest autumn/winter salad mix,
Brussels sprouts, cabbages, carrots,
cauliflowers, celery, chard, leeks, mizuna,
mustard spinach, pak choi, parsnips, radishes,
rocket, spinach, turnips
Keep adding waste to the runner-bean trench
Plant bare-rooted fruit bushes, garlic, shallots
Protect mizuna, mustard spinach, pak choi,
spinach, spinach beet, radicchio, rocket

Late autumn is a quiet time in the kitchen garden, although any hard frosts will mean that crops such as the parsnips and the trench celery have that added boost of sweetness and flavour. Other crops, including the winter salads and early sowings for next spring, will benefit from some protection. If possible, it's worth uncovering them on milder days and covering them up at night when frost is forecast.

In the garden

Beans and peas

Broad beans Sown under cloches in early October, these should be sturdy little plants by now.

Peas The peas sown last month should also be through by now.

Runner-bean trench Carry on adding kitchen waste to the trench. When you have covered the bottom with about 5cm (2in) of organic matter, cover it lightly with some of the soil you dug out. Carry on over the next few months, adding layers of kitchen waste and soil until the trench is full – probably in early spring. Then leave it for two months to settle before sowing or planting out young bean plants next year in late May.

Brassicas and leafy greens

Brussels sprouts Carry on harvesting the sprouts as you need them, but save some for Christmas!

Cabbage White and red cabbages don't like hard frost, so, if there is a danger of any, cut cabbages that are ready for harvesting and store them in a cool, dry place. Remove any damaged outer leaves and put them in net bags so that the air can circulate around them. Keep the remaining cabbages under horticultural fleece.

Cauliflowers Harvest any remaining late varieties.

Chard Carry on picking.

Spinach Harvest leaves that are large enough under the cloche, but mostly, it will be ready early next year.

Spinach beet Keep protected for a spring crop.

English essential Cabbages can be grown into the autumn and are a familiar sight in any kitchen garden

Attractive choice

Far right You can pick and eat the baby leaves of turnips or leave the roots in the soil until the turnips are ready

Right Many splendoured chard – ornamental and edible

Bulbs, roots and stems

Carrots Continue to harvest any late varieties.

Celery The chances are there will have been some hard frosts by now. Harvest the celery heads as you need them.

Garlic You can plant more garlic this month unless the soil is waterlogged or frozen.

Leeks Carry on harvesting the leeks, as needed.

Parsnips Harvest, as required, either by digging them from the soil or, if you lifted the whole crop earlier, take them from the boxes of compost where they are stored.

Radishes If you sowed any winter radishes in late summer, they should be ready for harvesting this month. You can also use the leaves as a cut-and-come-again crop – they have a peppery flavour.

DELIA IN THE KITCHEN Celery

Celery is as English as the Stilton cheese it's often partnered and perhaps enjoyed best of all with: fresh, crunchy and crisp with a good cheese board, some fresh-shelled walnuts and a glass of vintage port. To prepare celery, first of all remove the tough, large outer stalks and, as these are usually distinctively stringy, take a sharp paring knife and pare off the strings. Now trim off the outer skin around the root and cut the head vertically so that some of the sweet, edible root is still intact, then cut into 6-8 layered, vertical strips ■

Shallots Like onions, the easiest way to grow shallots is from sets – small bulbs. Some varieties can be planted in autumn when there is more room in the kitchen garden while others are best planted out in mid or late winter or even early spring. Check on the labels for the best variety to plant now.

Make drills about 4cm (1½in) deep – the tips of the shallots should just show above the soil – and set them about 15cm (6in) apart in rows 30cm (12in) apart. The birds take great pleasure in just pulling them out of the soil, so trim any loose skin at the tips to make it harder for them.

Turnips Harvest quick-growing turnips that were sown during September.

Oriental greens

Mizuna, mustard spinach and pak choi Use these as cut-and-come-again crops this month, taking a few leaves at a time.

Alternatively, if you have left the oriental greens to grow on, you can harvest whole plants now by cutting them off at the base. Protect them with horticultural fleece or a cloche.

Enter shallots
Far left The easiest way to grow shallots is to plant them in sets – small bulbs – similar to those of onions

Left The tips should just protrude above the soil

Salad leaves

Autumn/winter salad mix Pick leaves as they are ready.

Radicchio Under a cloche this will continue to grow slowly. The small leaves of the deep purple-red varieties should be starting to show traces of that colouring now.

Rocket Pick individual leaves and keep the crop protected.

Soft-fruit bushes

This is the best month to plant bare-rooted fruit bushes. These are plants that are dug out of the ground when they are dormant and sold with no compost around their roots. They are cheaper than container-grown plants and easier to send by mail order. Prepare the soil as for container-grown fruit (see page 44).

Blackcurrants To encourage plenty of new growth from below soil level, these need to be planted 5cm (2in) deeper than they were previously growing in the nursery.

Gooseberries Plant in a generous-size hole in which some well-rotted organic matter has been incorporated at the bottom.

Raspberries Trim away the longest roots on the canes to

about 20cm (8in). Then, with the roots well spread out, plant the bushes about 40cm (16in) apart along the row, at the same depth as the soil mark on the stems (this shows the depth at which they were grown in the nursery) to encourage plenty of new growth from below soil level. Firm them well with the toe of your boot and cut all the canes back to about 30cm (12in) from the ground.

Redcurrants Treat as you do for gooseberry bushes but, as they dislike water-logging, if your soil is heavy, work a spadeful of grit into the bottom of the hole as well.

In the greenhouse

Salad leaves

Autumn/winter salad mix If you sowed a salad mix in the empty cucumber growing bags during October, make sure that the compost doesn't dry out.

DELIA IN THE KITCHEN Turnips

In winter, turnips are less tender than during the summer, and can be steamed and mashed to a purée with an equal amount of steamed potatoes, with the addition of a little cream and butter. I love them sliced wafer thin in Cornish pasties and roasted as a vegetable. To prepare turnips, all you need here is to use a potato peeler to peel them in precisely the same way as a potato, slicing off the root end first with a knife. Then just cut the turnips into suitably-sized chunks to steam or roast ■

November

Braised Celery Vinaigrette

Serves 6

Celery is a wonderful vegetable for serving with poultry or game birds. This particular recipe can be served hot with a main course or at room temperature with cold cuts and salads.

3 heads celery
425ml (15fl oz) hot vegetable stock
150ml (5fl oz) dry white wine
1 clove garlic, slightly crushed
a strip of lemon zest
¼ teaspoon celery seeds
salt and freshly milled black pepper

For the vinaigrette
3 tablespoons olive oil
1 tablespoon lemon juice
2 rounded tablespoons chopped fresh parsley
½ teaspoon mixed pepper berries, crushed

You will also need a large, flameproof casserole with a well-fitting lid.

Begin by trimming the heads of celery back to 15-18cm (6-7in) in length. Shave off the base of each head, and it may be necessary to strip off 2 or even 3 of the outer stalks if they're coarse or damaged (don't worry – all respectable trimmings can be used for stock or soup). Now cut the heads into quarters lengthways and rinse them well in cold water, then drain them and arrange in a flameproof casserole (preferably one that can take the celery arranged flat in one layer). Now add the stock, wine, garlic, lemon zest and celery seeds plus a little freshly milled black pepper. Bring all this up to simmering point, then insert a double layer of greaseproof paper into the casserole so that it sits directly on top of the celery and comes 2.5cm (1in) or so up the sides. Cover with a well-fitting lid and continue to simmer gently until the celery is tender – this will take about 1 hour, but do be sure it is tender because celery can be very deceptive and it is the one vegetable that should not be served *al dente*!

When it is tender, use a draining spoon to remove the celery and arrange it in a shallow serving dish. Then briskly boil the juice remaining in the casserole (without a lid) until reduced to only some 2 or 3 tablespoons. Now remove the casserole from the heat and stir in all the vinaigrette ingredients. Taste and season with salt, then pour the sauce over the celery. Serve warm there and then, or else cooled to room temperature.

Spiced Roast Parsnips Chunks
with Coriander Chutney

Serves 2-3 as a snack or accompaniment

'Never dig parsnips till there's been a good hard ground frost.' That emphatic statement was instilled upon me as a child by my grandfather and I now know he was right. Frost quite definitely sharpens up all the lovely fragrance and flavour of parsnips. During the long winter months when little else but stored roots are available on the kitchen garden front – what we need are lots of varieties in the way we cook them. This one's a winner – lovely to serve as a starter preceding a curry or alongside it as an accompaniment.

570g (1lb 4oz) parsnips, peeled
½ teaspoon whole cumin seeds
½ teaspoon whole coriander seeds
1 clove garlic, peeled
2 rounded teaspoons Madras curry paste
2 tablespoons groundnut or other flavourless oil
¾ teaspoon sea salt

For the coriander chutney
25g (1oz) fresh coriander leaves
2 tablespoons lime juice
1 fresh green chilli, halved and deseeded
1 clove garlic, peeled
1 tablespoon natural yoghurt
½ teaspoon golden caster sugar
salt and freshly milled black pepper

Pre-heat the oven to gas mark 6, 200°C (400°F).

You will also need a medium baking tray,
25.5 x 35cm (10 x 14in).

Begin by making the chutney, by simply whizzing everything together in a blender, then pour into a bowl and leave aside for the flavours to develop. Now cut the parsnips into 5cm (2in) lengths that are about 2cm (¾in) at the thickest end. Then place the salt and garlic in a mortar and crush them together; as the garlic comes into contact with the salt, it will quickly break down into a purée. Then add the cumin and coriander seeds and crush those too, but not too finely. Now add the curry paste and the oil and give everything a good whisk together. Next, put the parsnips into a medium mixing bowl and add the spice paste, tossing everything together to give the parsnips a good coating. Now tip the parsnips on to the baking tray, spread them out and bake on the centre shelf for 30 minutes. Serve them hot, dipping each one into the chutney before eating.

Stir-fried Green Vegetables
Serves 4

This is the classic Chinese fry first, steam second, which results in a fragrant crunchiness.

110g (4oz) cauliflower
175g (6oz) broccoli
2 medium leeks
4 spring onions, trimmed
275g (10oz) pak choi
5cm (2in) piece root ginger, peeled
2 tablespoons groundnut or other flavourless oil
2 cloves garlic, peeled and thickly sliced
3 tablespoons Japanese soy sauce
75ml (3fl oz) Shaosing brown rice wine,
or dry sherry
1 dessertspoon golden caster sugar

To garnish
2 spring onions, finely shredded
½ medium red chilli, deseeded and cut into fine shreds

First, prepare the vegetables: the cauliflower should be separated out and cut into tiny florets, and the same with the broccoli. Wash and trim the leeks, then halve and thinly slice them, while the spring onions should be sliced into matchsticks, as should the ginger. Finally, cut each head of pak choi into 6 wedges through the root.

To cook, heat the oil over a high heat in a wok or large frying pan, add the the ginger and garlic and fry for 10 seconds, then add the cauliflower and broccoli and stir-fry for 1 minute. Next, add the leeks and stir-fry for another minute.

Add the spring onions and pak choi, toss it all together, then add the soy sauce, rice wine (or dry sherry), 75ml (3fl oz) water and the sugar. Reduce the heat to medium, put a lid on, and cook for 4 minutes, stirring occasionally. Serve the vegetables with the spring onions and chilli sprinkled over.

Winter

December

Traditional Brussels sprouts and parsnips are at their best – perfect for Christmas fare

Winter is now officially here, and this is another quiet month in the kitchen garden, with crops such as Brussels sprouts, parsnips and celery ready to make a home-grown contribution to the Christmas feast. During December hardy leafy vegetables, such as chard and some of the oriental leaves, make a valuable fresh addition to the recommended five portions of fruit and vegetables a day. While they are hardy, they can get somewhat battered by the winter weather, so a little protection with cloches is a good idea.

TASKS FOR DECEMBER

Harvest autumn/winter salad mix, Brussels sprouts, carrots, celery, chard, herbs, leeks, mizuna, mustard spinach, pak choi, parsnips, radicchio, radishes, rocket, turnips
Keep adding waste to the runner-bean trench
Plant garlic
Protect autumn/winter salad mix, broad beans, fig and peach trees, mizuna, mustard spinach, pak choi, peas
Sow cabbages, cauliflowers

In the garden

Beans and peas

Broad beans and peas Just check that the cloches are firmly secured. Gales at this time of year can easily dislodge the lighter plastic kinds and a blast of icy air on previously protected seedlings does them no good at all.

Runner-bean trench Carry on adding kitchen waste to the trench through the month.

Brassicas and leafy greens

Brussels sprouts Keep harvesting the sprouts from their stems or trees.

Chard Continue to use the brightly coloured stems and leaves through the winter.

Spinach and spinach beet The remaining crops won't be ready to pick until spring.

DELIA IN THE KITCHEN Brussels sprouts

To cook Brussels sprouts, there's no need to make incisions in the stalks. All you need to do for 450g (1lb) of sprouts is take off the outer leaves if they look a bit weary (if not, leave them on), sprinkle with salt and steam them for 5-8 minutes, depending on their size, but watch carefully and remember undercooking is just as bad as overcooking, so use a skewer to test when they're tender. Another way to serve them is to have a frying pan with ½ a teaspoon of butter and ½ a teaspoon of oil very hot, then, after giving them about one minute's less steaming, toss them around in the hot pan to finish cooking and to turn them fairly brown at the edges ■

Winter cheer Beautiful leafy chard, with shining foliage and stems of red, yellow, purple and pink, lives up to its name of Bright Lights

Under cover

Top left Broad beans thriving in the cloche

Top right Peas growing under a tent cloche

Below left Parsley in a pot in the greenhouse. Give your herbs plenty of water to keep them going in the winter

Below right Coriander nurtured in a pot in the greenhouse

Bulbs, roots and stems

Carrots Pull the last of any late varieties.

Celery Harvest the celery heads as you need them. Don't forget that during spells of drier weather, watering well before you harvest the stalks helps to keep them crisp.

Garlic You can plant more cloves of garlic this month unless the soil is waterlogged or frozen.

Leeks Continue to harvest the fresh leeks, as needed.

Parsnips Pull up the parsnips or use from boxes of compost.

Radishes Harvest winter radishes and their peppery leaves.

Shallots Check that the birds haven't pulled out of the soil the sets that were planted last month, as they do out of sheer devilment! If they have, it's better to re-plant the sets in a new hole, rather than simply pushing them back down into the soil. If you do this, you may damage the base plate and this can cause diseases to set in.

Turnips Harvest the last of the turnips now.

Oriental greens

Mizuna, mustard spinach and pak choi Carry on enjoying the greens as cut-and-come-again crops, or mature plants.

Salad leaves

Autumn/winter salad mix If you still have some autumn/winter leaves, keep them protected and pick the last of them as and when you need them to brighten winter salads.

Radicchio Early sowings may be ready for harvesting.

Rocket Pick any remaining leaves from under the cloche.

Fruit trees

Apricots Apricot trees, unlike peach (or nectarine) trees, don't need protecting over the winter except in colder gardens.

Figs Since figs take one to two years to crop well, in cold gardens it is worth protecting embryo figs over the winter months with straw, conifer prunings or bracken that is held in place with netting, which can be fixed to the vine eyes used for the training wires.

Peaches Protect wall-trained peaches (and nectarines) from peach-leaf curl (a fungal disease the spores of which are carried in water droplets) and from frost. It is also advisable to keep the fruit buds dry so they are less likely to rot.

One simple way is to fix large hooks to the wall or fence well

above the tree, and then, having stapled or tacked a sheet of clear polythene large enough to cover the tree, to a stout pole, hang it from the hooks. Leave the sides open to allow air to circulate.

Herbs

Rosemary, sage, thyme Keep picking the evergreen herbs.

In the greenhouse

Brassicas and leafy greens

Cabbages Sow these in modules or Jiffy 7s and leave in a heated propagator. They will be ready to plant outside under cloches in late winter after hardening off. Sow only half a dozen or so now, and perhaps another half dozen in January. That way, you will stagger the cropping time, rather than winding up with a glut.

Cauliflowers Sow early summer varieties in modules or Jiffy 7s at the end of the month, to plant out in late winter/early spring.

Salad leaves

Autumn/winter salad mix Make sure the compost does not dry out and pick leaves, as required. Although you can get several pickings from each plant, they will not go on for ever!

Herbs

Chives, coriander, mint, parsley Keep the pots of herbs in the greenhouse moist, but not waterlogged, and pick as needed.

Withstanding frost
Above left Grown under a cloche a few weeks ago, radicchio will soon be ready for harvesting

Above right Protecting peaches from frost with a sheet of clear polythene, leaving the sides open for the air to circulate

December

Caramelised Cheese and Onion Tartlets

Makes about 8

These are a splendid offering for vegetarian guests at any party. You can make the cases and the filling in advance, then just put them together and bake them on the day. Serve them warm from the oven.

For the cheese pastry
75g (3oz) butter, at room temperature
175g (6oz) plain flour
50g (2oz) strong Cheddar cheese, grated
½ teaspoon mustard powder
a pinch of cayenne pepper

For the filling
25g (1oz) butter
2 large onions, finely chopped
2 large eggs, beaten
½ teaspoon mustard powder
175ml (6fl oz) single cream
75g (3oz) Gruyère cheese, grated
cayenne pepper
salt and freshly milled black pepper

You will also need an 8-hole patty tin, with cups, 2 x10cm (¾ x 4in), greased, and a 13cm (5in) pastry cutter.

Pre-heat the oven to gas mark 4, 180°C (350°F).

First, make up the pastry by rubbing the butter lightly into the flour, then adding the cheese, mustard and cayenne, plus just enough cold water to make a smooth dough. Then place the dough in a polythene bag to rest in the fridge for 20 minutes. After that, roll it out as thinly as possible and use the cutter (or a saucer) to stamp out 8 rounds. Line the tin with them, then pre-bake in the oven for 15-20 minutes or until the pastry is cooked through but not too coloured. Then cool them on a wire rack and store in an airtight tin until needed. Meanwhile, for the filling, melt the butter in a pan and cook the onions very gently, stirring often, for 30 minutes or until they are a lovely golden-brown caramel colour. Leave to cool.

To bake the tartlets: brush a little beaten egg on each pastry case and bake them (same temperature as above) for 5 minutes – this helps to provide a seal for the pastry and stops it becoming soggy. Now mix the beaten eggs with the mustard and cream in a jug and season with salt and pepper. Next, spoon the onion mixture into the cases and top that with grated cheese.

Finally, pour in the egg mixture and sprinkle with a little cayenne. Bake for 30 minutes or until puffy and golden. Stand in the tin for 10 minutes and serve warm.

Soup Flamande with Crème Fraîche and Frizzled Sprouts

Serves 8

This classic soup from Brussels is so creamy and subtle that even determined sprout haters will succumb to its charms.

350g (12oz) potatoes
2 large leeks, trimmed
350g (12oz) Brussels sprouts
2 rounded tablespoons crème fraîche
50g (2oz) butter
425ml (15fl oz) hot vegetable stock
570ml (1 pint) milk
a squeeze of lemon juice
salt and freshly milled black pepper

To garnish
8 large sprouts, trimmed and shredded
2 tablespoons olive oil
4 tablespoons crème fraîche

Start by peeling and thickly slicing the potatoes. When the leeks are trimmed and washed, cut them all the way through vertically; then chop them into 2.5cm (1in) pieces. Then trim the bases of the sprouts and discard any damaged outer leaves and quarter the larger sprouts and halve any smaller ones. Next, melt the butter in a good, large saucepan, add the potatoes, leeks and sprouts, and stir well to coat them nicely in the butter. Add some salt and freshly milled black pepper, turn the heat to low, put a lid on and allow the vegetables to sweat gently for 5 minutes. Then add the stock and milk, bring everything up to simmering point and cook very gently for 20-25 minutes, or until the potatoes are soft. Because of the milk it's best to put the lid only three-quarters on to prevent everything boiling over and keep the heat really low.

After that, liquidise the soup and then return it to the pan; add the 2 rounded tablespoons of crème fraîche, then re-heat the soup gently, taste and add a good squeeze of lemon juice and more seasoning, if it needs it.

For the garnish, heat the olive oil in a medium frying pan over a high heat and, when the oil is shimmering, add the shredded sprouts and fry them, stirring occasionally, so they don't catch on the base of the pan. When they are crisp and golden brown (2-3 minutes) lift them, using a draining spoon, on to crumpled kitchen paper to drain. Serve the soup in hot bowls with a little crème fraîche spooned on top, garnished with the frizzled sprouts.

Quick Stir-fried Spiced Red Cabbage with Apples

Serves 2

Red cabbage is wonderfully versatile – you can cook it long and slow and it seems to go on improving, or in the recipe below: fast cooking to retain some crunchiness and bite.

225g (8oz) red cabbage
1 medium Cox's apple, cored but not peeled
25g (1oz) butter
2 teaspoons oil
1 small onion, chopped
2 cloves garlic, chopped
¼ teaspoon each ground cloves and cinnamon
a few gratings of whole nutmeg
1 teaspoon brown sugar
1 tablespoon red wine vinegar
salt and freshly milled black pepper

First, you need to shred the cabbage quite finely into 5mm (¼in) shreds, discarding any tough stalky bits (including the root). Chop the apple quite small too but leave the skin on (it improves the flavour).

Now in a large, heavy-based frying pan melt the butter and oil over a medium heat, then stir in the onion and cook it for 2-3 minutes before adding the apple and garlic. Continue to cook for 2-3 minutes, then turn the heat up to high, add the cabbage and stir-fry it by keeping it on the move with a wooden spoon, so that it all comes into contact with the heat at the base of the pan.

After 5 minutes or so it should have shrunk a bit, so at this point sprinkle in the spices and a seasoning of salt and pepper, then turn the heat down and let it go on cooking for a further 10 minutes, stirring it once or twice during that time. Bite a piece to see if it's tender and, when it's ready, turn the heat up again, sprinkle in the sugar and vinegar. Stir everything thoroughly, then serve.

January

The kitchen garden is in mid-winter mood and there are a few jobs to do in the greenhouse

TASKS FOR JANUARY

Harvest autumn/winter salad mix, chard, herbs, leeks, mizuna, mustard, spinach, pak choi, parsnips, radicchio, radishes
Keep adding waste to the runner-bean trench
Plant cauliflowers, garlic
Protect beans, cabbages, fig and peach trees, mizuna, mustard spinach, pak choi, peas, radicchio, radishes, spinach, spinach beet
Sow cabbages, calabrese, cauliflowers, radishes

A new year but not quite yet a new season in the kitchen garden. Some of the winter root vegetables are still hanging on – the celery, leeks and the parsnips, but the Brussels sprouts and oriental greens are coming to an end, as is the chard. The beans and peas should be growing well, still protected from the worst of the weather under cloches and in the greenhouse – sowing more spring cabbage and hardening off the first of the brassicas for next spring. You can even try planting some cauliflower seedlings in pots as we did.

In the garden

Beans and peas

Broad beans and peas Keep checking that the young plants are protected from the frost and wind. In Delia's kitchen garden we learnt the hard way how important that is when, in January, the early sowings of beans and peas took a bit of a battering after strong cold winds whipped the cloche off them and left them exposed for a day or two. The broad beans survived but we had to replace the peas with some sown in the greenhouse in a length of plastic guttering.

Runner-bean trench Carry on filling up the trench, adding layers of kitchen waste and soil.

Brassicas and leafy greens

Brussels sprouts These will be coming to an end this month. As each stalk has finished (all the Brussels sprouts have been picked from it), dig it up. After that, you can then chop up the stalk with a spade before adding the debris to the compost bin.

Chard You should still be able to enjoy chard, although the crop will be coming to an end. As the plants become exhausted, pull them up, roots and all and add them to the compost bin.

Spinach and spinach beet Keep them protected.

Bulbs, roots and stems

Celery Any celery still left in the ground should be dug up now. Although celery can tolerate the cold, it starts to deteriorate when the ground is wet as well – it is the combination of the wet and the cold that most plants hate.

Garlic There is still time to plant some more garlic, providing the soil is not frozen or too waterlogged. If it is, you can start the garlic off in the greenhouse – sow it in modules, ready to plant out in the spring. It will just mean that it is ready later than garlic planted directly outside before Christmas.

Leeks Carry on pulling the leeks.

Parsnips Harvest the roots, either from the ground or from the boxes or trays of sand where you have stored them.

Radishes Carry on enjoying the winter radishes. At the end of the month, sow a half row of summer radishes between the beans and peas. Normally, you wouldn't sow radishes until next month but, with the additional warmth under the cloche protecting the beans and peas, the radishes should get off to a flying start, giving you a crop early in the year.

Shallots Sets planted in November should have sprouted now, and, with luck, have become of less interest to the birds.

Oriental greens

Mizuna, mustard spinach and pak choi Under a cloche you may still find some leaves to harvest, but the oriental greens will be coming to an end now as late winter approaches.

Salad leaves

Radicchio Harvest the plants growing under the cloche now as a cut-and-come-again crop.

Fruit trees

Figs and peaches Check that the protection given to the peach and fig trees in December is still in place.

In the greenhouse

Brassicas and leafy greens

Cabbages As soon as the cabbages sown in December have become sturdy little plants, start to harden them off. Sow some more spring cabbages now to stagger cropping.

Cauliflowers You can plant a couple of the seedlings out into 25.5cm (10in) terracotta pots now, if you like, to grow in the greenhouse. We did this as an experiment, and they were a great success. Keep the other cauliflower seedlings to plant out later on next month for harvesting in the spring.

Salad leaves

Autumn/winter salad mix The plants will be more or less exhausted, but if you have any leaves left, harvest them now.

After that, remove any remaining stumps or stems from the growing bag and empty the leftover compost on to a garden border.

Herbs

Chives, coriander, mint, parsley All these herbs should be growing well inside, although some, such as coriander, may have initially got off to a slow start. We found it took a while for coriander to germinate but it grew well once it had got going.

In Delia's greenhouse, the Italian flat-leafed parsley grew particularly well. When using herbs from pots, it's best to pick a few leaves evenly across the plants, rather than denude one or two.

Greenhouse effect
Above left Cauliflower seedlings doing well in a pot during winter

Above right Shallots sprouting successfully

DELIA IN THE KITCHEN Parsnips

What an absolute star a parsnip is – full of soft, juicy flesh and fragrant, sweet flavour. They are lovely plain, steamed, mashed and roasted. I like them best after the frosts have arrived, which really does intensify their flavour. Small, young parsnips don't need peeling and coring; the older, larger, late-winter parsnips need the peel taken off and the cores cut out. Then cut them into even-sized pieces and steam for 10-15 minutes, and serve with plenty of salt and freshly milled black pepper and a little butter. For roasting, prepare them in the same way, toss in a little oil and season. Place on a pre-heated roasting tray and roast in the oven pre-heated to gas mark 7, 220°C (425°F) for 30-40 minutes, depending on the size of the parsnip. 450g (1lb) of parsnips will serve 4 people ■

January

Root Vegetable, Cheese and Onion Pot Pie

Serves 4-6

A pot pie is nothing more than homely comfort food and January is the perfect month to feature it after the rich excesses of the Christmas feasts. You can vary the vegetables by replacing celery with celeriac or swede with other roots, and I think some very fluffy creamy mashed potato – Irish-style, with cabbage and spring onions and lots of butter – would be a splendid accompaniment.

225g (8oz) each carrots, swede and celery, peeled and cut into 2.5cm (1in) chunks
450g (1lb) leeks, washed and trimmed, halved lengthways and cut into 5cm (2in) thick chunks
110g (4oz) Lancashire cheese, crumbled
a little freshly grated nutmeg
1 egg, beaten, to glaze
salt and freshly milled black pepper

For the Parmesan pastry
25g (1oz) finely grated Parmesan
110g (4oz) plain flour,
plus a little extra for dusting

a pinch of salt
25g (1oz) softened lard
25g (1oz) softened butter

For the cheese, onion and sage sauce
50g (2oz) Lancashire cheese, crumbled
25g (1oz) Parmesan, finely grated
1 medium onion, finely chopped
1 dessertspoon finely chopped fresh sage
40g (1½oz) butter
40g (1½oz) plain flour
570ml (1 pint) milk
a little freshly grated nutmeg
1 tablespoon wholegrain mustard
salt and freshly milled black pepper

You will also need a round baking dish with a diameter of 23cm (9in), 5cm (2in) deep.

First of all, place all the prepared carrots, swede, celery and leeks in a steamer. Pour in some boiling water from the kettle, add the freshly grated nutmeg and some salt, then cover and steam the vegetables for about 20 minutes. When the thickest parts of the root vegetables feel tender when tested with a skewer, tip them all into a large bowl and allow them to cool.

Meanwhile, make the sauce and the pastry. For the sauce, in a smallish saucepan, melt the butter and add the onion and, when you've stirred it so it's nice and buttery, let it cook on the lowest possible heat for about 20 minutes. It's important not to let it colour, so give it a stir from time to time.

Now, using a wooden spoon, stir in the flour until smooth, then add the milk a little at a time, switching to a balloon whisk, and whisking well after each addition. Now season the sauce with nutmeg and salt and freshly milled black pepper to taste, and let it barely simmer for 5 minutes. After that, stir in the wholegrain mustard, the cheeses and the sage. Then, leave to cool.

To make the pastry, first sift the flour with the pinch of salt into a large bowl, holding the sieve up high to give it a good airing. Then add the lard and butter and, using only your fingertips, lightly and gently rub the fat into the flour. When everything is crumbly, add the Parmesan and then sprinkle in some cold water – about 1 tablespoon. Start to mix the pastry with a knife and then finish off with your hands, adding more drops of water till you have a smooth dough that will leave the bowl clean. Then pop the pastry into a polythene bag and let it rest in the fridge for 30 minutes.

When you are ready to bake the pie, pre-heat the oven to gas mark 7, 220°C (425°F). Carefully mix the steamed vegetables with the sauce and pile half the mixture into the dish. Now sprinkle half the crumbled Lancashire cheese over the top and then repeat with the remaining mixture and cheese. Next, roll the pastry out into a 30cm (12in) circle on a surface lightly dusted with flour and, as you roll, give it quarter turns to keep the round shape. After you have cut the round, roll out the trimmings and cut a 1cm (½in) strip to go around the edge of the dish. Now dampen the edge of the dish with water and place the strip of pastry around the rim, pressing down well. Dampen the strip and then transfer the circle of pastry, rolling it over the pin, to the dish and press it lightly and firmly over the edges to seal. Next, using the blunt side of a knife, knock up the edges, then flute them using your thumb to push out and your forefinger to pull in again. Now make a hole in the centre of the pastry lid to let the steam out, and brush the surface with beaten egg. Finally, place the dish on the baking sheet and bake it for 25 to 30 minutes on the centre shelf or until the pie is bubbling hot and the pastry is golden brown and crusty.

Roasted Roots with Herbs

Serves 4

This is always going to be an easy option if you're entertaining, as all the vegetables get cooked without any attention. One thing I have found invaluable, too, is being able to prepare them well ahead, which gives you that organised feeling. This is a particularly lovely combination of vegetables, but you can vary it to whatever is available.

4 small whole carrots
4 small whole parsnips
½ swede (about 150g/5oz),
cut into 2.5cm (1in) wedges
1 small turnip, cut in half
and then into 2cm (¾in) slices
2 medium red onions,
cut through the root into quarters
2 Desirée potatoes (150g/5oz each), cut into 6 wedges
1 fat garlic clove, crushed
3 tablespoons olive oil
1 tablespoon chopped mixed fresh herbs
(including thyme, rosemary and sage)
salt and freshly milled black pepper

You will also need a large, solid baking tray,
30 x 40cm (12 x 16in).

Pre-heat the oven to gas mark 9, 240°C (475°F) .

First, scrub the carrots and parsnips, dry them well and place them in a large bowl with all the other prepared vegetables. Now add the crushed garlic, olive oil and mixed herbs; then, using your hands, mix well to make sure they all have a good coating of the oil.

You can leave them like this covered with clingfilm for up to 2 hours until you are ready to cook them – in which case the oil will have nicely absorbed the flavour of the garlic and herbs. When you're ready to cook the vegetables, arrange them on the baking sheet, sprinkle with salt and a good grinding of freshly milled black pepper. Cook them in the pre-heated oven on a high shelf for 35-40 minutes or until they are cooked through and turning brown at the edges.

February

Winter is on its way out and the welcome months of spring are just around the corner

TASKS FOR FEBRUARY

Harvest herbs, leeks, parsnips, radicchio, radishes, sprouting broccoli
Keep adding waste to the runner-bean trench
Plant cabbages, garlic, shallots
Protect broad beans, Brussels sprouts, cabbages, carrots, fruit trees and bushes, lettuces, peas, radishes, strawberries, turnips
Sow aubergines, broad beans, Brussels sprouts, cabbages, calabrese, carrots, chillies, herbs, leeks, lettuces, parsley, peas, radishes, spinach, sweet peas, sweet peppers, tomatoes, turnips

While there is not much left in the kitchen garden now, there is a definite sense of gearing up for the coming season with seed sowing underway in the shelter of the greenhouse. Outside, any empty beds where crops will be sown or planted out that are not yet protected with cloches should be covered now with black polythene – it really does warm up the soil and can bring crops forward by a couple of weeks or more.

In the garden

Beans and peas

Broad beans and peas The broad beans and peas will continue to grow well under the cloche. Sow another double row of each crop directly into the soil, which has been warmed with polythene and, once they have germinated and spring is here, treat in the same way as last spring/summer.

Runner-bean trench Carry on adding kitchen and garden waste to the trench and covering each layer with soil, ready to plant the beans in May.

Brassicas and leafy greens

Brussels sprouts Warm up the soil for a couple of weeks by covering it with black polythene. Then, using one end of the bed as a seedbed, sow a row of Brussels sprouts. Sow thinly in a drill 2cm (¾in) deep and, afterwards, cover with a cloche or a double thicknesses of horticultural fleece. You can transplant them in April into their final positions for harvesting from September onwards.

Cabbages Plant out under horticultural fleece or cloches. Since some can be pulled for spring greens before they have hearted up, plant them closer together – about 15cm (6in) apart – with a view to pulling alternate ones. Harden off the young plants for a week or two before planting out, although they will still benefit from the protection of a double layer of horticultural fleece or even a cloche until the weather warms up.

Gearing up Getting ready for the coming season with plenty of new seedlings underway in the greenhouse

Spinach and spinach beet In pre-warmed soil, sow a part-row of spinach and cover it with fleece. Sow the rest of the row in a couple of weeks' time. Leave last season's crops under the protection of the cloche until next month when you can start to pick the leaves.

Sprouting broccoli The sprouting broccoli sown in March will be ready for harvesting this month and next.

Bulbs, roots and stems

Carrots For an early crop of carrots, sow a row, under the protection of horticultural fleece or a cloche. If you have had problems with carrot fly in the past, it's best to keep thinning to a minimum (it's the smell released when carrots are disturbed that attracts the pest), so sow very meanly, or use seed tape (see page 18).

Garlic There is just about time to plant garlic now and next month, if you haven't already done so. Garlic does need a period of cold weather to develop well, so it may not be quite as successful as earlier plantings, since the worst of the winter is now over.

Leeks and parsnips Harvest any remaining leeks and parsnips now and dig the beds over at the end of the month.

Radishes Harvest winter radishes. If the half row of summer radishes sown under the cloche between the beans and the peas last month are up, sow another half row now to keep the supply going.

Shallots Plant some more sets now. After each new planting check regularly, to see that the birds haven't pulled them up.

Turnips Sow a part-row at the end of the month and protect it with fleece. These will be ready to harvest from early summer.

Salad leaves

Lettuces Under the protection of the cloche, sow another part-row of a hardy lettuce variety for the spring.

Radicchio Harvest any remaining radicchio.

Soft-fruit bushes

Raspberries Mulch container-grown bushes, planted last year, with 10cm (4in) of well-rotted organic matter to help root the stubs of established canes and encourage new growth from below the soil. Prune autumn-fruiting raspberries – cut all the canes back to soil level.

Strawberries Towards the end of February, check any strawberry plants that were planted out and, if there are signs of new leaves coming through, trim the old leaves that have protected the crown of the plant from the worst of the winter weather. Allowing light and air to the crown will encourage the new growth to be vigorous and healthy. For the best results, sprinkle some sulphate of potash at the rate of 15g/¾oz to 1 sq m/10.8sq ft. If you cover the plants with cloches or fleece now you will bring the crop forward by a week or two in summer. Once the flowers start to form, remove, or at least open the cloches during the day, to let the pollinating insects in.

Soft fruit in pots

Blueberries Prune out any dead wood and, if the compost feels dry, start watering at the end of the month.

Strawberries As the plants in pots start to grow again at the end of the month, if the weather has not been too cold, begin to water them. Trim off any old leaves remaining from last season.

Fruit trees

Peaches If you haven't already protected peaches (or nectarines) with polythene during the winter months, cover them with horticultural fleece, as the fruit buds begin to swell. Not only will it help guard against frost, it will also keep off the bullfinches. These birds can be a real menace, stripping a peach tree of its fruit buds, resulting in no crop in the summer.

If you have any other fruit trees or bushes in the garden that are not in a fruit cage, protect those now, too, for the same reason.

In the greenhouse
Brassicas and leafy greens

Cabbages Start sowing some more summer cabbages in modules or Jiffy 7s to plant out in March and April. Harden the seedlings off as they are ready, before planting them out under horticultural fleece or cloches.

Calabrese Towards the end of the month, start sowing calabrese in modules or Jiffy 7s, ready for hardening off next month and planting out in early April.

Cauliflowers Towards the end of the month, harden off the seedlings sown in December, to go out under cloches or fleece.

If you potted up some cauliflowers in the greenhouse during January, they should be growing very well inside and even starting to produce some florets.

Looking forward
Far left Calabrese seedlings ready for hardening off

Left Planting calabrese in a module

Sprouting broccoli Although much slower-growing than calabrese, sprouting broccoli is a useful vegetable to have in the garden in the months when there is little else. Sow in modules or Jiffy 7s, to harvest early next spring. You should be able to pick the sprouting broccoli sown in March last year this month and next.

Bulbs, roots and stems

Leeks Sow leeks in modules or trays, ready for planting out from April onwards.

Fruiting vegetables

Aubergines, chillies and sweet peppers At the end of February, sow in pots or Jiffy 7s, then place in a heated propagator.

Tomatoes Sow tomatoes to be grown in the greenhouse at the end of the month. Sow in modules or Jiffy 7s and place them in a propagator. If you are planning to grow tomatoes outside, it is too early to sow them now.

In Delia's garden, as well as the superbly flavoured Sungold and Gardener's Delight, and old favourites Ailsa Craig and

Harbinger that we grew successfully in the first season, we decided to try some other varieties for the second season – Italian Cuor di Bue and Red Pear Franchi – for salads and cooking.

Herbs

Chives, coriander, mint, parsley Keep the herbs in pots cropping as long as possible, then discard the plants. Sow some coriander and parsley in modules, ready to go outside in the spring.

Lettuces Sow some in trays or modules every two weeks or so, to give you an earlier crop than seed sown directly under cloches from now on. Lettuces sown now will be ready to go out next month.

Flowers

Sweet peas Sow these seeds now in root trainers or pots, to be planted with runner beans later in the year (see page 35).

DELIA IN THE KITCHEN Sprouting broccoli

After the lean winter months, the first fresh green vegetable to herald spring is sprouting broccoli, with its purple or white flowery heads. It has a lovely, sweet, very green kind of flavour and tender stalks. I like to eat the leaves, stalks and heads when it's very young. Steam them, sprinkled with salt, for 3-4 minutes. You will need 110g (4oz) per person ■

February

Potatoes Boulangères with Sage

Serves 8

Potatoes Boulangères – so named because French bakers would offer to bake people's potatoes in their ovens after the bread was baked – are crisp and golden on the top, soft and creamy within.

1.15kg (2lb 8oz) Desirée potatoes, peeled

1 heaped tablespoon finely chopped fresh sage,

plus 8 small sage leaves

2 medium onions

275ml (10fl oz) hot vegetable stock

150ml (5fl oz) milk

40g (1½oz) butter

a little olive oil, for dipping

sea salt and freshly milled black pepper

You will also need an ovenproof dish, 20 x 28cm (8 x 11in) and 5cm (2in) deep, lightly buttered.

Pre-heat the oven to gas mark 4, 180°C (350°F).

Begin by peeling and cutting the onions in half and then the halves into the thinnest slices possible; the potatoes should be sliced, but not too thinly (about 3mm/⅛in thick). Now all you do is arrange a layer of potatoes, then onions, in the dish, followed by a scattering of chopped sage, then season. Continue layering in this way, finishing with a layer of potatoes that slightly overlap. Now mix the stock and milk together and pour it over the potatoes. Then put little flecks of butter all over the top and place the dish on the highest shelf of the oven for 1 hour, by which time the top will be crisp and golden. Dip the sage leaves in the olive oil and scatter them over the top 10 minutes before the end of the cooking time.

Slow-cooked Root Vegetable Soup

Serves 6

Something happens to vegetables when they're cooked very slowly for a long time: their flavour becomes mellow but at the same time more intense, and your kitchen is filled with aromas of goodness. This soup is also completely fat-free.

Vegetable quantities are prepared weights

225g (8oz) peeled carrots, cut into 5cm (2in) lengths

225g (8oz) peeled celeriac, cut into 5cm (2in) pieces

225g (8oz) trimmed and washed leeks, halved and cut into 5cm (2in) lengths

225g (8oz) peeled swede, cut into 5cm (2in) pieces

1 small onion, roughly chopped

1.5 litres (2½ pints) hot vegetable stock

3 bay leaves

salt and freshly milled black pepper

To serve

6 teaspoons fat-free Greek yoghurt

a few fresh chives, snipped

You will also need a lidded, flameproof casserole
with a capacity of 3.5 litres/6 pints.

Pre-heat the oven to gas mark 1, 140°C (275°F).

There's not much to do here once everything is peeled and
chopped. All you do is place everything in the casserole and bring it
up to a gentle simmer, then put the lid on, place it in the lowest part
of the oven and leave it there for 3 hours, by which time the
vegetables will be meltingly tender. Next, remove the bay leaves and
process or liquidise the soup in several batches to a purée, then
gently re-heat, and serve the soup in bowls with a teaspoon of Greek
yoghurt swirled into each and garnished with the fresh chives.

Leek and Soured Cream Flan

Serves 4-6

This flan has a crisp, cheesy wholemeal pastry and makes
a very good lunch dish with a salad.

For the pastry

75g (3oz) self-raising flour

75g (3oz) plain wholemeal flour, plus extra for dusting

a pinch of salt

¾ teaspoon mustard powder

40g (1½oz) pure vegetable fat or lard

40g (1½oz) softened butter

50g (2oz) Cheddar, finely grated

For the filling

1.35kg (3lb) leeks

150ml (5fl oz) soured cream

50g (2oz) butter

1 clove garlic, crushed

2 tablespoons double cream

1 large egg, beaten

50g (2oz) Cheddar, grated

salt and freshly milled black pepper

You will also need a 23cm (9in), loose-bottomed,
fluted tart tin, 4cm (1½in) deep, lightly greased,
and a small, solid baking sheet.

To make the pastry, sift the flours, salt and mustard powder
into a large bowl, then rub in the fats until the mixture resembles
fine breadcrumbs, lifting everything up and letting it fall back into
the bowl to give it a good airing. Now stir in the cheese, and add
enough cold water, about a tablespoon, to make a dough that leaves
the bowl clean. Pop the pastry into a polythene bag and leave to rest
in the fridge for 30 minutes. Meanwhile, pre-heat the oven to gas
mark 4, 180°C (350°F), and put the baking sheet in to pre-heat as
well. Now for the filling. First, prepare the leeks. Begin by making a
vertical split about halfway down the centre of each one and clean
them by running them under cold water while you fan out the
layers. Then slice them in half lengthways and leaving 4cm (1½in) of
green on the ends, slice them thinly.

Now melt the butter in a large pan, add the leeks and garlic,
and some seasoning. Cover and cook gently, without browning, for
10-15 minutes or until the juice runs out of them. Then you need to
transfer them to a large sieve set over a bowl to drain, placing a
saucer with a weight on top of them to press out every last drop.

Next, roll out the pastry on a lightly floured surface and line
the tin with it, using any surplus pastry to reinforce the sides and
base and carefully smoothing it into place. Now prick the base all
over with a fork (to prevent it rising), then bake the flan case in the
centre of the oven on the baking sheet for 15 minutes.

After that, remove from the oven and brush all over with a
little beaten egg (from the filling ingredients). Return to the oven
for 5 minutes more, then remove and turn the heat up to gas mark 5,
190°C (375°F). Now return the leeks to the pan. Combine the
soured cream and double cream with the remaining beaten egg, and
then stir this into the leek mixture, seasoning to taste. Spread the
mixture over the pastry case, sprinkle with the cheese and bake in
the centre of the oven for 40 minutes or until brown and crispy.

Patio Garden

You can grow a range of produce in terracotta pots, which also looks attractive and stylish

VARIETIES

Chard Bright Lights
Chilli Cayenne or Jalapeño
Courgette Bambino F1
French bean Sultana
Garlic Rossa di Saluggia
Lambs' lettuce Jade
Potato (new) Charlotte
Runner bean Painted Lady Improved
Salad leaves – seasonal mixes
Strawberry Elvira
Summer squash Sunburst
Tomato Garden Pearl
Turnip Purple Top Milan

If you don't have room for a kitchen garden like Delia's, you can still grow a surprising amount of produce in machine-made terracotta pots, which come in a range of shapes and sizes, are cheap and can look stylish when painted. If space is very limited, plan so that one crop can follow another in the same pot. Use soil-based John Innes No 3 compost, or if weight is a factor (on a balcony), use a lighter weight compost mixed 50:50 with John Innes. For crops that have to be supported, you'll need some bamboo canes and, to start crops off indoors, some biodegradable pots or Jiffy 7s (see page 18) and some seed trays to stand them in. One of the best investments you can make is a small electric heated propagator. It will get all your seedlings off to a flying start, and as you only need relatively few plants of everything, it will be plenty big enough.

Spring

MARCH

Indoors

New potatoes Chit a couple of potatoes now (see page 35).

On the patio

Salad leaves Use a wide, shallow bowl (18cm/7in deep x 51cm/20in across the top) and fill it with compost. Then, with a 30cm (12in) ruler, mark out four shallow drills across the width, less than 1cm ($\frac{1}{2}$in) deep, watering along each one. Some packs of salad leaves mix up all the varieties, while others come in separate packets. With the latter, you can sow individual rows, or mix them before you sow. Sow meanly and cover the drills with compost. The seeds should germinate within a week or so. Thin out the seedlings while they're very small – 1cm ($\frac{1}{2}$in) high, increasing the space between them to 2.5cm (1in) as they grow.

APRIL

Indoors

Chillies Sow in the same way as tomatoes (see below), but remember to wash your hands after handling the seeds. Once the plants are a reasonable size, pot them into their final pots – one per 20cm (8in) pot.

French beans Sow as many seeds as you need plants, plus a few spares, in case they don't all germinate. Eight plants will fit in a pot measuring 30cm (12in) in diameter across the top. Sow the seeds in Jiffy 7s (see page 18) and place them in a propagator. As soon as they germinate (4-6 days), remove them from the propagator. Put them into a plastic tray to make watering less messy and stand them on a sunny windowsill. They will lean towards the light as they grow, so turn them round 180° every day or two.

Once the beans have reached a height of 13-15cm (5-6in), fill the pot with compost. Push in ten 2m (6ft 6in) bamboo canes, as far as they'll go, spacing them evenly around the edge of the pot. Gather the canes together at the top and tie with twine to form a wigwam.

Plant each plant beside a cane, and push a couple of bean seeds into the compost by the two empty canes. These will be a few weeks behind the plants and so prolong your cropping season. Water well.

Tomatoes Decide how many plants you want and, for each plant, sow two or three seeds per Jiffy 7 or small pot 1cm (½in) deep. Place them in a propagator. As soon as the seedlings appear, take them out, and remove all but the strongest seedling. Put them in a plastic tray and treat them as you would the beans. When the plants are 7.5cm (3in) tall, plant them in compost in 30cm (12in) diameter pots – three to a pot – and keep them inside.

On the patio

New potatoes Put 10cm (4in) of compost in a large pot. Lay two 'chitted' potatoes, shoots pointing upwards, spaced out on top. Cover with 5-7.5cm (2-3in) of compost. If it is dry, water well.

The pot will only be about a third full. As the potatoes produce green shoots, add more compost, leaving 10-15cm (4-6in) of the shoots clear. This is earthing up, container style (see page 58). Keep the compost moist, but it shouldn't be soggy or the tubers may rot.

Strawberries Plant four or six plants (see page 46) in a 30cm (12in) pot in a 75% multipurpose compost/25% fine grit or perlite mix. Keep the compost moist – overwatering will cause the roots to die.

MAY

Indoors

Chillies Treat as you would the tomatoes (see below, left).

Courgettes/summer squashes Sow in Jiffy 7s or pots.

French beans On warm days take them outside to harden off. At the end of May, leave them out full time. If a cold spell is forecast, drape a piece of fleece over them. Keep well watered – every day in warm, dry weather, and every other day in cooler weather – even if it rains, as the leaves act as umbrellas so very little rain water reaches the compost. Feed weekly with well-diluted tomato fertiliser.

Runner beans Sow in pots or trays. Towards the end of May, harden them off – take them outside on warm days and bring them in at night. After about a week, so long as the night-time temperature does not fall below 10°C (50°F), leave them out all night.

Tomatoes Harden them off, and, at the end of the month, leave them outside. Water well, and feed weekly with tomato fertiliser.

On the patio

New potatoes When the compost is 3cm (1¼in) from the top of the pot, stop earthing up. Keep the compost moist.

Salad leaves Once the plants are 5-7.5cm (2-3in) high, start to pick one or two leaves from individual plants or cut a whole plant, leaving the stump in place to produce more leaves.

Strawberries As they flower, feed weekly with tomato fertiliser until the berries form. If there's any threat of frost, cover with fleece. Cover berries with netting or an upside-down hanging basket to deter birds.

Summer

JUNE

On the patio

Chillies Treat as tomatoes.

Courgettes/summer squashes Transfer the plants to a large pot, filled with compost enriched with a little pelleted chicken manure. Plant deeply – up to the seed leaves – to give the plant support.

French beans These should be cropping well. Once the plants have reached the top of the canes, pinch out the growing point on each one and water thoroughly every day. Watch out for blackfly. If you have a small invasion, use a hand sprayer filled with water and a squirt of washing-up liquid to get rid of them.

New potatoes Keep watering well during flowering. Towards the end of June, scrape aside some compost – if the tubers are the right size, start to harvest. The easiest way to do this is to tip the contents into a wheelbarrow or on to a sheet of polythene.

Runner beans Re-use the potato pot, fill it three-quarters full with fresh compost and mix in a handful of pelleted chicken manure. Add more compost to within a few centimetres of the top. Push in eight 2.4m (8ft) tall bamboo canes, evenly spaced around the edge. Pull them together at the top and tie with twine. Plant one bean plant beside each cane, and encourage the young growth around it.

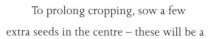

To prolong cropping, sow a few extra seeds in the centre – these will be a few weeks behind the pot-grown beans. If the weather is very hot, you might prefer to sow some extra French beans instead – they don't mind the hot weather. Keep well watered.

Salad leaves Keep on harvesting and sowing more. At this time of year, everything germinates very quickly and easily.

Strawberries Start to pick and eat.

Tomatoes Towards the end of June, you will be able to harvest the first small tomatoes. Bush varieties don't need staking, but you can put three short canes around the rim of the pot and loop soft twine between them to provide near-invisible support. Later on, you will be surprised at how the weight of the crop can pull the plants down almost to the ground. Keep them well watered.

JULY

On the patio

Chillies Water and feed as for tomatoes.

Courgettes/summer squashes This should be a large plant now. Put in a cane or two and tie the main stem to it, or put an empty flowerpot or hanging basket upside down underneath the stems to keep them off the ground. Towards the end of July, start to harvest.

French beans Keep on harvesting and watering. Feed them once a week with a weak solution of tomato fertiliser.

Runner beans If the weather is unusually hot and dry, the plants will produce plenty of flowers but many will drop off before they turn into beans. Some gardeners recommend spraying the flowers with water to encourage 'setting', but the problem is high night-time temperatures. Keep the compost watered and wait for the nights to cool down. You may have to wait a little longer for your beans.

Salad leaves Harvest and sow a few seeds where there are gaps.

Strawberries If the plant produces runners, cut them off unless you want to increase your stock of plants (see page 75).

Tomatoes Harvest daily and keep on watering, and feed weekly.

AUGUST

On the patio

Chard Sow individual multigerm seeds (in small clusters) in a large pot. Mark out rows 7.5cm (3in) apart in a grid, and sow the seeds 2.5cm (1in) deep where the lines cross. If you are plagued with squirrels, an empty hanging basket, upside down, over the top of the pot will help to stop them digging. Or, stretch a piece of enviromesh over the pot, tied under the rim, until seedlings emerge.

Chillies If you like your chillies a little milder, harvest them while they are green. If you like them hotter, leave them to turn red. Water and feed as you would tomatoes.

Courgettes/summer squashes Start to harvest.

French beans Carry on picking and keep watered and fed. At the end of August cropping may ease off. Cut the stalks at soil level, remove the canes and untangle the growth. Leave the roots in the compost as this adds nitrogen, which benefits leafy crops, such as chard, which you can sow now – see above.

Runner beans Keep picking and water at least once a day.

Salad leaves Few plants will allow you to cut-and-come-again more than four times. Pull out the stumps and re-sow with an autumn/winter salad mix. Sow thinly in drills about 1cm (½in) deep and 15cm (6in) apart. Cover to keep the squirrels at bay.

Tomatoes Keep harvesting every day, as well as watering regularly and feeding once a week.

Turnips Fill a 30cm (12in) pot with compost and sow seed in drills 2cm (¾in) deep and in rows 15cm (6in) apart.

Autumn

SEPTEMBER

On the patio

Chard Pick evenly across the pot so that you don't denude individual plants. Keep the upside-down basket over the plant.

Chillies Pick as required. Before the first frosts, harvest them all or take the whole plant out of the pot, shake off the soil and hang it upside down to dry. Pick the chillies as you need them.

Courgettes/summer squashes The plant will be more or less exhausted, so take it out of the pot, replace the used compost with fresh, and re-sow with another winter hardy crop.

Runner beans Keep harvesting, although the plants will start to wind down. Water daily and feed weekly.

Salad leaves Harvest, again picking across the whole pot, rather than from just one or two plants.

Tomatoes These should still be cropping well through the first part of September. Later in the month, as the nights get colder, they will slow down.

OCTOBER

On the patio

Chard Carry on picking the leaves.

Garlic In a 30cm (12in) pot, plant four cloves, evenly spaced, 10cm (4in) deep. Take off the papery skin from each clove, making sure you don't damage the base plate (the flat bit).

Lambs' lettuce Station-sow two or three seeds 1cm (½in) deep, 10cm (4in) apart, in rows 15cm (6in) apart in a 30cm (12in) pot. Protect with horticultural fleece or a bell cloche on top of the pot.

Runner beans These will have finished cropping by now. Cut off the stalks at soil level and remove the top growth. Clean the canes and store them for next year. Nodules on the bean roots add nitrogen, beneficial for leaf growth, so leave them in the compost and re-sow with another crop.

Salad leaves Harvest the autumn/winter mix as baby leaves.

Tomatoes Any green tomatoes can be picked and kept in a warm place to ripen. Remove the plants and dispose of the compost – if you don't have a garden to put it on to, it can go to the tip for recycling. Fill the pot with fresh compost and plant another crop.

Turnips Thin the seedlings out to 10cm (4in) apart. You can harvest the turnips for the roots or the leaves (the leaves taste like spicy greens) – but not both.

NOVEMBER

On the patio

Chard Pick and cover with a cloche or horticultural fleece.

Garlic This should be starting to shoot now.

Salad leaves Harvest and, as for chard, protect in cold weather.

Turnips Protect with a cloche or horticultural fleece.

Winter

DECEMBER

On the patio

Chard A little protection will result in a few new young leaves.

Garlic The shoots should be a few centimetres tall. Despite its Mediterranean associations, garlic is tough and needs no protection.

Lambs' lettuce and salad leaves There will still be a few leaves to add freshness to a stir-fry or bought salad.

Turnips If you like turnips to be the size of a large marble you could harvest a few now. Or, pick the leaves.

JANUARY

On the patio

Chard, lambs' lettuce and salad leaves Pick any remaining leaves. They will be finishing, so pull out the plants.

Garlic Keep the compost moist. As the weather warms up, the bulbs will need ample water to swell, ready to harvest in June/July.

Turnips Continue to harvest.

FEBRUARY

On the patio

Apart from garlic and any turnips grown for their roots, it is time to start the patio garden cycle again. The terracotta pots need emptying; dispose of the compost – on to a border or take it to the tip. Scrub the pots and re-paint them so they're ready when you're sowing spring crops.

Square foot garden

Create a neat plot in a simple frame and grow crops in succession all year round

Calabrese Trixie F1
Carrot Early Amsterdam Forcing 3
Chard Bright Lights
Chervil (or flat-leaf parsley/coriander)
French bean Cobra
Garlic Rossa di Saluggia
Lambs' lettuce Jade
Lettuce Little Gem
Pak choi Riko F1
Peas Feltham First
Potato (new) Charlotte
Radish French Breakfast
Rocket Apollo and Runway
Salad leaves – seasonal mixes
Shallot Mikor
Spinach Lazio
Spring cabbage Hispi F1
Spring onion Eiffel
Tomato Sungold F1
Turnip Atlantic

Another way to enjoy the delights of fresh, home-grown food, wherever you have room in a border, is to create a Square Foot Garden. The idea, which comes from America (hence 'Square Foot' and not 'Square 30 Centimetres'), involves growing a crop in a square foot of soil – salad leaves are a prime example, as are radishes, spinach and tomatoes. You can have as many squares as you have room for and in any configuration. An ideal size is 4ft x 4ft, giving 16 squares. Obviously, this is not going to feed a family of four but, for an individual or a couple, it will certainly provide enough produce to make the whole exercise worthwhile.

While you can simply designate an area within a border, it's simpler to create a simple wooden frame to keep the bordering plants at bay. A 4ft square garden can be made from 4ft lengths of 6 x 1in timber, screwed to four pointed stakes, 1 x 1 x 12in, one at each corner, then pushed into the ground. If you get the local timber merchant to cut the wood for you, the only tool you need to put the frame together is a screwdriver. Stain the wood with an opaque wood stain, and then, to make it easy to work out the squares, hammer galvanised tacks into the wood at 1ft intervals all the way round. When you are sowing, you simply line up your ruler (a 30cm/12in ruler is ideal) with the relevant two tacks, then press it into the soil to mark the squares. Or, you could mark the frame at 12in intervals with a permanent marker.

Where space is so limited, you have to make the soil work hard. So, as soon as one crop has been harvested, sow the square with another, or, better still, start some crops on the windowsill inside. After tomatoes have

PLAN FOR FOUR SEASONS

TOMATOES | CALABRESE | FRENCH BEANS | PEAS
NEW POTATOES | LETTUCES | CARROTS | RADISHES
SPINACH | SPRING ONIONS | SALAD LEAVES | GARLIC
PAK CHOI | ROCKET | CHERVIL | SALAD LEAVES

GARLIC | SHALLOTS | SHALLOTS | LAMBS' LETTUCE
PAK CHOI | AUTUMN/WINTER SALAD LEAVES | BABY TURNIPS | RADISHES
SPINACH | AUTUMN/WINTER SALAD LEAVES | SPRING CABBAGE | GARLIC
PAK CHOI | CHARD | AUTUMN/WINTER SALAD LEAVES | SPINACH

Spring/Summer

Autumn/Winter

Seasonal fare
Far left For spring and summer, you can grow favourites such as new potatoes and try more unusual crops from pak choi to rocket

Left Baby turnips and shallots are ideal for autumn/winter and you'll have plenty of mixed salad leaves all through the year

finished cropping in mid-September, for example, the square can be re-planted with garlic. You can also grow up, as well as along, so climbing French beans are a better bet than dwarf, and a cordon tomato (one grown up a cane) makes better use of the space than a bush tomato would.

Salad leaves of various kinds work well because you can 'cut-and-come-again', as do quick-growing crops, such as radishes. It's fun to plant a single potato tuber through an X-shape cut in a square of black polythene – it saves on earthing up, for which there would be no room. Some plants are not suitable – a courgette would dominate not just its own square but its neighbours' squares as well!

Here, more than ever, grow what you like to eat – we have suggested a square of chervil for its slightly aniseed flavour (you only get the odd leaf or two in a mixed salad bag), but you could substitute flat-leaf parsley or coriander.

Make a simple frame and cover it with horticultural fleece early in the season to bring crops on, replacing it with enviromesh to deter pests later on.

All squared up
Above left A corner showing the squares marked out
Above right Sowing seeds in drills within the square

Preparing the soil

With such a small area producing crops non-stop through the year, you need to add some nutrients to the soil before sowing – lightly work three slightly heaped spadefuls of well-rotted compost into the top few inches. As all the crops are annuals (germinating, growing and being harvested in one season), they need only about 15cm (6in) of good soil, apart from the potatoes, which do push down further.

Sowing

Check on the seed packets to see what the spacing should be for each crop, then mark your rows within the relevant square, using the ruler to make shallow grooves in the soil about 1cm (½in) deep. Sow seeds sparingly, so you'll have less thinning to do. If the soil is dry, carefully water the drills before sowing. Cover them with dry soil. If the seedlings are too close, with one hand, press down the soil on either side of the surplus seeds, using your index and middle fingers, then tease them out with the index finger and thumb of the other hand.

Varieties & Suppliers

Below are the varieties we used in Delia's kitchen garden, chosen for flavour. Seed-to-harvest times in italics are a guide. Times vary with the variety, the weather and where you live. In warm conditions, seeds germinate quicker and seedlings grow faster than when it's cold. Opposite, is a list of useful suppliers to get you started

Recommended varieties

Vegetables

Asparagus *2-3 years*
  Theilim F1
Aubergine *16-24 weeks*
  Long Purple

Beetroot *7-13 weeks*
  Boltardy
Borlotti bean *16-24 weeks*
  Lingua di Fuoco
Broad bean *12-16 weeks*
(*28-35 weeks for autumn-sown crops*)
  Aquadulce
Broccoli *32-48 weeks*
  Claret F1
  Early White Sprouting
  Tenderstem Green
  Inspiration F1b
Brussels sprouts *20-32 weeks*
  Maximus F1

Cabbage *20-34 weeks*
  Hispi F1 (spring greens/summer)
  Ormskirk Late 1 (Savoy) (autumn/winter)
  Red Flare F1 (autumn/winter red)
  Red Fuego F1 (summer red)
  Rodima F1 (autumn/winter red)
Calabrese (green sprouting broccoli) *11-14 weeks*
  Tiara
Carrot *9-20 weeks*
  Autumn King
  Early Amsterdam Forcing 3
  Flyaway F1
Cauliflower *16-40 weeks*
  All The Year Round (summer/autumn)
  Andes (summer/autumn)
  Galleon (winter)

Patriot (early summer)
  Snow Crown (summer)
Celery (trench) *32-36 weeks*
  Giant Red (self-blanching) *12-16 weeks*
  Golden Self Blanching
Chard *8-12 weeks*
  Bright Lights
Chilli *20-28 weeks*
  Cayenne
Courgette *10-12 weeks*
  Eight Ball F1
  Gold Rush F1
Cucumber *14-16 weeks*
  Sweet Crunch F1

Dwarf French bean *8-13 weeks*
  Masterpiece

Garlic *20-36 weeks*
  Rossa di Saluggia

Leek *16-20 weeks*
  Musselburgh

Lettuce *4-16*
  All The Year Round
  Cosmic
  Lobjoits
  Tom Thumb

Mizuna *8-10 weeks*
Mustard spinach *5-12 weeks*
  Komatsuna

Onion *18-20 weeks*
36-38 weeks (for autumn-sown crops)
  Hyduro
  Red Baron

Pak choi *5-8 weeks*
  Choko F1
  Riko F1
Parsnip *16-26 weeks*
  Hollow Crown
Peas *11-13 weeks*
  Delikett
  Feltham First

Potato *14-20 weeks*
  Belle de Fontenay (salad/late)
  Desirée (maincrop)
  International Kidney (new early)
  Pink Fir Apple (salad/late)
Pumpkin *20-28 weeks*
  Oz

Radicchio *9-16 weeks*
  Rosso di Treviso 2
  Variegated Palla Rossa di Chioggia
Radish *4-6 weeks*
  April Cross F1
  Black Spanish Round
  French Breakfast
  Minowase (mouli) (autumn/winter)
  Munchen Bier
Rocket *3-6 weeks*
  Apollo
  Runway
  Selvatica

Runner bean *12-24 weeks*

   Painted Lady Improved

Shallot *18-36 weeks*

   Longor (from sets)

Spinach *5-12 weeks*

   Hector F1

   Samish F1

   San Marco F1

Spinach beet *5-12 weeks*

   Perpetual

Spring onion *6-10 weeks*

   Parade

   Toga

   White Lisbon Winter Hardy

Sweetcorn *10-15 weeks*

   Bodacious

   Minipop

Sweet pepper *24-28 weeks*

   Corno di Torro Rosso

   Sweet Delight

Tomato *16-24 weeks*

   Ailsa Craig

   Cuor di Bue

   Garden Pearl

   Gardener's Delight

   Harbinger

   Red Pear Franchi

   Sungold

Turnip *6-10 weeks*

   Golden Ball

   Tokyo Cross F1

Fruit trees

1-2 Years

Apricot

   Prunus

   'Moor Park'

   Prunus

   'NL Early'

Fig

   Ficus carica 'Brown Turkey'

Peach

   'Duke of York'

   'Peregrine'

Soft-fruit bushes

Blackcurrants

   Ben Connan

   Ben Sarek

Blueberries

   Blue Crop

   Goldtraub

Gooseberries

   Invicta

Raspberries

   Autumn Bliss (autumn-fruiting)

   Glen Lyon (summer-fruiting)

Redcurrants

   Red Lake

   Rovado

Rhubarb *1-2 years*

   Early Champagne

Strawberry *8-20 weeks*

   Elvira

   Florence

   Gariguette

   Hapil

   Mara des Bois

Note F1 hybrids are specially bred for high quality, good cropping and also, for disease resistance. They do not come true from seed, so you will need to buy fresh each year.

Suppliers

Fertiliser and potting compost

Trans-organic

01359-240529;

www.trans-organic.co.uk

Seeds, plants and fruit trees

Chiltern Seeds

Flower, fruit, salad and vegetable seeds, including uncommon varieties

01229-581137;

www.chilternseeds.co.uk

DT Brown

Flower, fruit, vegetable seeds

0845-6014656

www.dtbrownseeds.co.uk

Johnsons

Flower, herb and vegetable seeds

01638-552200

www.johnsons-seeds.com

Ken Muir

Fruit and flowers; specialist in strawberry, including frozen plants, plus equipment

0870-7479111;

www.kenmuir.co.uk

Mr Fothergill's

Flower, fruit, herbs, vegetables seeds and plants, including asparagus crowns

01638-552512;

www.mr-fothergills.co.uk

Seeds of Italy

Seeds for Italian flowers, herbs, salads and vegetables

020 8930-2516;

www.seedsofitaly.com

Suttons

Vegetable, flower and fruit seeds

0870-2202899;

www.suttons-seeds.co.uk

The Organic Gardening Catalogue

Seeds and plants for flowers, fruit, herbs, salads and vegetables for organic gardening

0845-1301304;

www.organiccatalogue.com

Thompson & Morgan

On-line seed and plant supplier of flowers, herbs, shrubs and vegetables

01473-688821;

www.thompson-morgan.com

Unwins

Supplier of seeds for flowers and vegetables; also fruit trees

01945-588522;

www.unwins-seeds.co.uk

Trained fruit

Crown Nurseries

Specialist fruit-tree nursery

High Street, Ufford, Suffolk

IP13 6EL

01394-460755;

www.crown-nursery.co.uk

Keepers Nursery

Specialist fruit-tree nursery

Gallants Court, East Farleigh, Maidstone, Kent, ME15 0LE

01622-726465;

www.keepers-nursery.co.uk

Trees for Life

For stockist of trained fruit, visit: www.trees-for-life.com

Garden tools and accessories

Baileys Home and Garden

Modern and vintage garden tools and accessories

01989-561931; www.baileyshomeandgarden.com

Earthworks London

Accessories, including Foxgloves, gloves made in colourful, stretchy fabric that makes them comfortable to work with

07721-398082;

ew@earthworkslondon.com

NuCan

Watering can with a push button, allowing you to open and shut the spout so you can control the flow

01983-822588;

www.nucan.co.uk

RK Alliston

A range of stylish gardening and lifestyle accessories

0845-1305577;

www.rkalliston.com

Two Wests & Elliott Ltd

Greenhouse equipment, plant protection and fruit cages

01246-451077;

www.twowests.co.uk

Useful websites

For general gardening advice, and for further information on pests and diseases, here are two helpful websites:

www.bbc.co.uk/gardening/advice

www.rhs.org.uk

Index